THE
Parent's
HANDBOOK

Systematic Training for Effective Parenting

Don Dinkmeyer, Sr.
Gary D. McKay
Don Dinkmeyer, Jr.

American Guidance Service, Inc.
Circle Pines, Minnesota 55014-1796
1-800-328-2560

To all the parents and leaders of STEP, and to Rudolf Dreikurs—our teacher, friend, and source of encouragement.

Together, we are meeting our responsibility and challenge: Parent education is the right of every child.

Matt Keller, *Marketing Director*
Mary Kaye Kuzma, *Purchasing Agent*
Charles Pederson, *Associate Editor*
Marjorie Lisovskis, *Writer/Editor*
Evans McCormick Creative, *Page and Cover Design*
John Bush, *Cartoons*

Chapter 1: The four goals of misbehavior originated in Rudolf Dreikurs and Vickie Soltz, *Children: The Challenge* (New York: Dutton, 1987).

Chapter 2: Stepsibling information is from Don Dinkmeyer and Gary D. McKay, *Raising a Responsible Child, Revised* (New York: Fireside, 1996); demanding, can't standing, complaining, and blaming are from Gary D. McKay and Don Dinkmeyer, *How You Feel Is Up to You* (San Luis Obispo, CA: Impact, 1994) and Albert Ellis, *How to Stubbornly Refuse to Make Yourself Miserable About Anything—Yes, Anything!* (Secaucus, NJ: Lyle Stuart, 1988).

Chapter 4: I-messages come from Thomas Gordon, *P.E.T.: Parent Effectiveness Training* (New York: NAL-Dutton, 1975); "I noticed" statements come from Jane Nelson, Lynn Lott, and H. Stephen Glenn, *Positive Discipline A-Z* (Rocklin, CA: Prima, 1993).

Chapter 5: Problem ownership is from Thomas Gordon, *P.E.T.: Parent Effectiveness Training* (New York: NAL-Dutton, 1975); problem-solving steps originated with Rudolf Dreikurs and Loren Grey, *A Parent's Guide to Child Discipline* (New York: Hawthorn, 1970); the job jar is from Don Dinkmeyer and Gary D. McKay, *Raising a Responsible Child, Revised* (New York: Fireside, 1996); ideas on single-parent families and stepfamilies are from Don Dinkmeyer, Gary D. McKay, and Joyce L. McKay, *New Beginnings* (Champaign, IL: Research Press, 1987).

Chapter 7: Information on schoolwork and logical consequences comes from Don Dinkmeyer and Gary D. McKay, *Raising a Responsible Child, Revised* (New York: Fireside, 1996); ideas on gangs are from Don Dinkmeyer and Gary D. McKay, *Raising a Responsible Child, Revised* (New York: Fireside, 1996) and Jane Nelson, Lynn Lott, and H. Stephen Glenn, *Positive Discipline A-Z* (Rocklin, CA: Prima, 1993).

Photo Credits: Cover: Steve McHugh, The Photography Group; Chapter 1: Michael Pole, Westlight; Chapters 2, 4-7: Cheryl Walsh Bellville; Chapter 3: Frozen Images.

Printed in the United States of America

ISBN 0-7854-1188-7

Product Number 16202

A 0 9 8 7 6 5 4 3

Contents

Other works by the authors

The Effective Parent (Don Dinkmeyer, Gary D. McKay, Don Dinkmeyer, Jr., James S. Dinkmeyer, and Joyce L. McKay)

Parenting Teenagers: Systematic Training for Effective Parenting of Teens (Don Dinkmeyer and Gary D. McKay)

Parenting Young Children: Systematic Training for Effective Parenting of Children Under Six (Don Dinkmeyer Sr., Gary D. McKay, James S. Dinkmeyer, and Don Dinkmeyer, Jr.)

Systematic Training for Effective Teaching (STET) (Don Dinkmeyer, Sr., Gary D. McKay, and Don Dinkmeyer, Jr.)

Preparing Responsible and Effective Parents (PREP) (Don Dinkmeyer, Sr., Gary D. McKay, Don Dinkmeyer, Jr., James S. Dinkmeyer, and Jon Carlson)

Time for a Better Marriage (Don Dinkmeyer and Jon Carlson)

Raising a Responsible Child: How to Prepare Your Child for Today's Complex World (Revised 1996) (Don Dinkmeyer and Gary D. McKay)

Taking Time for Love: How to Stay Happily Married (Don Dinkmeyer and Jon Carlson)

The Encouragement Book (Don Dinkmeyer and Lewis E. Losoncy)

The Skills of Encouragement (Don Dinkmeyer and Lewis E. Losoncy)

Leadership by Encouragement (Don Dinkmeyer and Daniel Eckstein)

How You Feel Is Up to You (Gary D. McKay and Don Dinkmeyer)

Consultation in the Schools (Don Dinkmeyer, Jr., Jon Carlson, and Don Dinkmeyer, Sr.)

New Beginnings (Don Dinkmeyer, Sr., Gary D. McKay, and Joyce L. McKay)

Introduction

We believe that being an effective parent is one of the most rewarding tasks in life. It is also one of the most challenging. Many conflicting theories of child training can be found in books, newspapers, and magazines, and on television. Our parents, friends, relatives, and spouses also have their own ideas. It's easy to become confused!

STEP *(Systematic Training for Effective Parenting)* provides a practical approach to raising children. *The Parent's Handbook* is your guide to a philosophy of child training that we and *more than three million parents* have found to be effective. STEP will work for you and your family, if you put into practice the ideas and skills presented in this book.

We suggest that you pace yourself by spending a week on each chapter. Read each chapter in the order presented. During that week, study the activities and charts in the chapter. Be sure to take time to carry out the activity titled "This Week." The activities "Just for You" and "For Your Family" will help you and your family.

Many parents choose to join a STEP parent education group. Tens of thousands of groups have given parents the opportunity to discuss ideas and share experiences.

When you study and apply the ideas, you will "graduate" as a more effective parent. If you're willing to stick with it, STEP will help you take your next good steps as a parent. The skills you learn can serve as guidelines in building a happy home.

Don Dinkmeyer Sr., Ph.D., Diplomate in Counseling Psychology, American Board of Professional Psychology; Diplomate, American Board of Family Psychology; Clinical Member, American Association for Marriage and Family Therapy

Gary D. McKay, Ph.D., Licensed Psychologist; Clinical Member, American Association for Marriage and Family Therapy

Don Dinkmeyer, Jr., Ph.D., Western Kentucky University; Licensed Marriage and Family Therapist

Understanding Yourself and Your Child

It's Wednesday night. Mom just picked up her children from school and day care. Now they are in the grocery store. Willie whines and rattles the cart. "I don't want baked beans. Yuck! I want macaroni and cheese!"

Keesha is tired and cranky. She has a cough and her nose is running. Mom is growing cranky too. Her head aches. She worries about what she'll do if Keesha gets sick and can't go to school tomorrow. She can't remember what she needs to buy for supper and hopes she has enough money to pay for it.

Keesha shoves her sister Becca into a stack of juice bottles. Plastic bottles roll all around. Becca shrieks and starts to cry. Mom takes a deep breath and closes her eyes. She asks herself, "Why does this have to be so hard?"

Most of us know how this mom feels. Every day we juggle work, children, money worries, and home tasks. Our time and patience are stretched thin. We want to do what's best for our families. Still, we can't quite figure out how. Often we feel overwhelmed and alone. But we don't need to be alone!

As parents, we have a common bond: our children. Most of us share a common goal: To raise children who are happy, healthy, confident, cooperative, responsible. To form strong, life-long family relationships. To help children grow into responsible adults. To raise a child who is loved and able to give love.

Here's what you will learn . . .

- Your parenting challenge is to raise a confident, responsible child.

- Your job is to guide—not to punish or do everything for your child.

- You can expect your child to cooperate.

- Your child's behavior always has a purpose.

- Your family can work, play, and grow together.

Parenting Skills Can Be Learned

The good news is that you *can* meet the challenges of parenting by:

- learning about how children grow and behave
- learning effective, positive ways to deal with misbehavior
- becoming skilled at encouraging your child
- discovering ways to listen and talk together openly

It's true that being a parent isn't easy. But what other important things in life are?

How did you learn to read? Did you just start reading? Or did someone else—a teacher, parent, sister, or brother—work with you to help you figure out the letters and sounds?

How did you learn to ride a bike? Did you simply get on and start pedaling? Or did someone hold onto the bike seat, offering tips and hints as you practiced?

It wasn't easy to learn to read or ride a bike. Each skill took effort, time, patience, and training. To learn it, you needed help.

Like reading or riding a bike, being a parent is a skill you can learn, practice, and improve.

The Important Job of Being a Parent

For many years children's teachers, counselors, and day-care providers have had training to do their jobs. Yet the idea that parents needed education to become better mothers and fathers was not widespread.

This is no longer true. Society has begun to value the job of parenting more and more. After all, parents are the most important people in children's lives!

You have many choices about how you want to raise your child. As you make these choices, the most important thing you can do is to keep in mind this parenting challenge:

- **to raise a child who is happy, healthy, confident, cooperative, and responsible**
- **to build a strong, lifelong relationship with your child**
- **to help your child grow to be a responsible adult**
- **to raise a loving and lovable child**

How Will STEP Help?

STEP can be your partner in making choices that are helpful for you and your child. This book shows a practical, *do-able* plan for you. It can help you find ways to meet the challenges of parenting, one step at a time. As you practice what STEP teaches, your skills and confidence will grow.

In this first chapter, you will learn about yourself by thinking about two questions:

- What do I like about what I'm doing?
- What do I want to change?

You will also learn some things about your child:

- What can I expect from my child?
- What traits in my child are special to me?
- Why does my child misbehave?
- How can I help my child make good choices about how to act?

And you will learn some ways to become closer as a family:

- How can we show that we love and respect each other?
- How can we have more fun together?

What Style of Parenting Will Help Me Meet My Goals?

You have a certain way of relating to your child. You can think of this as your *parenting style*. There are many styles of parenting. The three most common are:

- **Giving orders.** This style sets unreasonable limits. It gives children little or no freedom.
- **Giving in.** This style gives children lots of freedom but no limits.
- **Giving choices.** With this style, parents help children learn a balance between freedom and limits.

Let's look closely at these three styles. Few people follow one style only. Each of us tends toward one approach. As you read, think about your own parenting style. Ask yourself:

- How will my style help me meet the challenge of parenting?
- What can I change to help me meet the challenge?
- What are reasonable limits for my child? What is reasonable freedom?

Giving Orders

This style of parenting is often called *authoritarian*. The parents are strict. They set a lot of rules. The children are expected to obey the rules exactly. Often strict parents reward and punish children to keep them in line.

What Do Children Learn?

Rewards lead children to expect payment for "being good":

When Trahn was 7, his mother wanted him to keep quiet while the baby slept. As a reward, she gave him a can of soda. When he was 9, Mom needed Trahn to play with his little brother while she studied. As a reward, she let Trahn and his friend order pizza. Now Trahn is 11. His mother needs him to baby-sit after school. Trahn wants a reward: a CD player.

Children may follow strict rules to avoid conflict or punishment. In doing so, they may learn to please parents. They may also learn to be afraid of parents.

They may not learn to think for themselves. Instead, they may look to friends and others to tell them what to do. And friends don't always give sound advice.

Maureen is 8. She forgot her mittens at school. Her father yelled at her. The next day, Maureen forgot to bring home a permission slip about a field trip. Her dad was really mad. He told her, "No field trip for you!"

A few days later, Maureen got her report card. She saw check marks for "needs improvement." Maureen told her friend how mad her dad was going to be. Maureen's friend said, "Why don't you just erase the check marks?" Maureen thought that was a good idea.

When children are punished for "being bad," they may learn to resent parents. Often, they find a way to get even. Some children rebel against strict parents at an early age. Others may rebel as they grow older.

When children disobey, strict parents may sometimes yell, blame, or even hit their children. Children in turn feel helpless. They need to regain a sense of control. To do this, they may copy the parents' actions when they are with other children. They see that adults deal with problems loudly and violently. They may decide that yelling and hitting are the right ways to solve problems.

- Children need to trust, not fear, parents.
- Children need the chance to make choices. This will help them learn limits and responsibility.

Taking Stock

- How do you feel about being a parent? Think about how you feel right now.

- If you feel good, why? What are you doing that you feel good about? How can you keep that good feeling?

- Think of at least <u>one thing</u> that you feel good about today. Why is it good? How could you do more of that one good thing?

- Children need to see that calm words—not yelling or hitting—are the way to solve problems.

The authoritarian method doesn't help build trust. It doesn't offer freedom or choices. It doesn't teach children to use words to solve problems.

Giving In

Giving in is also called *permissive* parenting. Permissive parents set no limits or often change the limits they do set. Children grow up without consistent guidelines. The parents give in to whatever the children may want. We often say that these children are *spoiled*.

Freedom without limits usually means problems for everyone. Why? Because society sets limits. Children with no limits on their behavior will have trouble learning how to behave in our society.

What if there were no traffic rules? What if all drivers drove as they pleased? on the wrong side of the road? down the middle? without stopping? as fast as they chose? The results would be a lot of crashes. We couldn't call them "accidents" either!

Children with no limits may have trouble learning how to act with other people.

What Do Children Learn?

Without limits, children are likely to have more trouble, or "crashes," learning responsibility. They may have trouble getting along with others. They will usually learn to do as they please. They *won't* learn to care about the feelings and rights of others. They won't see that people have responsibilities to each other.

- Children need limits. These help them learn to make choices.
- Children need to know that other people are important too.
- If we want to raise children to become responsible adults, first we must help them to be responsible children. Setting no limits won't help us to meet the challenge of parenting.

Giving Choices

What approach to parenting *will* help us raise responsible children? Consider a *democratic* style. A democratic style isn't permissive. It balances freedom, or *rights*, and limits, or *responsibilities*. It aims to help children become responsible by doing two things:

- setting limits for children
- giving children choices within those limits

How do parents do this? Democratic parents encourage their children to make some decisions alone. They ask for their children's ideas about some family decisions too. This shows children that parents respect their opinions.

Kate is 11. She wants to sleep over at Briana's on Friday night. She wants to go to a movie with Ann and Yoki on Saturday night. Kate's dad says, "It's nice to have so many friends and plans. But two nights in a row are too much. You may either go out Friday or Saturday. You choose."

On Sunday afternoon, Vanessa and Leroy wanted to do something fun with their two children. They asked the boys to choose between the beach and the children's museum. Charles picked the beach. Ty picked the museum. The boys could not agree. Leroy said, "Sometimes it's hard to agree. How can we decide?" Ty said, "Let's draw straws." Charles said, "Okay." Leroy said, "The short straw will decide. Then next time, we'll do the other thing."

Giving choices is also a way to help children be more responsible.

Nine-year-old Corey would leave his muddy shoes on when he came inside. Dad said, "Corey, please remove your shoes, or you'll need to clean the tracks from the floor. You decide." One day, Corey didn't remove his shoes. So Dad handed him a sponge and a bucket of water. The next rainy day, Corey remembered to remove his shoes.

What Do Children Learn?

When children take part in decisions, they learn that their choices count. They also see that some choices carry responsibility. Does this mean that every decision is up to your child? No. It means that you involve your child in decision making where possible.

We want to teach our children to cooperate and be responsible. A democratic style of parenting can help us do that.

Later in STEP you will learn about some other ways to give choices. You will discover ways to discipline without rewards and punishment. You will see that misbehavior is a choice. You will learn ways to help children take responsibility for their choices.

Giving a Choice

Think of a choice you could offer your child. Be sure it is a choice you can accept. The choices will depend on your child's age and maturity. Here are some ideas:

- "For supper we can have pancakes or spaghetti. Which do you choose?"

- "You may choose any shirt that costs less than twelve dollars."

- "You may choose one of your card games for us to play tonight."

- "You have English and math homework. Which would you like to do first?"

What Can I Expect From My Child?

Before we can set limits and give choices, we need to decide what we can reasonably expect from our children. Each child is a unique mix of traits and behaviors. Some of these will not change. For example, a child is either a boy or a girl. Some children are more sensitive, some are stubborn.

Some traits may grow or lessen but will probably not go away. Some traits that we see today may change in a few weeks or months.

Other things, too, affect the way children grow and behave. Four important things are:

- temperament
- heredity and environment
- roles for boys and girls
- ages and stages

These things can confuse us as we try to understand how we can expect our children to act. Let's look at each one.

Temperament

Temperament means a style of behavior. Each child has an individual temperament. Temperament has nothing to do with how smart or talented a child is. It refers to the unique qualities a child is born with.

Some children are active, others are more calm. Some require lots of sleep, some less. Some like to be surrounded by people. Others like to be alone.

Maggie and Consuela are both 10. Maggie has a big group of friends. She loves to ride bikes, swim, and play kickball with them. Consuela likes puzzles and games. She and her friend Beth spend their free time at the library where they use the computer.

When we recognize and accept temperament, we gain understanding. This can help us enjoy our children. It helps us guide them in ways that suit them.

Heredity and Environment

Heredity refers to traits that "run in the family." These are traits a child is born with. Many physical traits are inherited, like eye color and height.

Some people believe behavior is inherited. Others believe it comes from a child's *environment*—the people, places, and events that a child experiences. Experts have debated this for many years:

- If behavior is inherited, why do children in one family act so differently?
- If it depends on environment, why do children act differently in the same situations?

Both heredity and environment play a part in how our children act. We can't change heredity. As we guide them, though, we can keep in mind that a child's environment is what we can most easily affect.

Joe is 8. His parents are divorced. Joe stays at his mom's one week and at his dad's the next. He makes the switch on Sunday nights. Joe enjoys both his parents. He is usually a happy boy. On Sunday mornings, Joe has started to act loud and mean. He argues and whines. He has temper tantrums and calls his parents names. He acts this way no matter where he is—Dad's home or Mom's.

Joe's mom and dad decide to talk with Joe. All three meet one night at a fast-food restaurant. Mom says to Joe, "It seems like Sundays have gotten pretty hard for you." Joe says, "I hate having to leave. I want to be with both of you." Dad says, "I'm sorry, Joe, but that isn't possible. Your mom and I still want to help, though. And we want to enjoy Sundays too. Would something make Sundays easier for you?"

Joe says, "I hate leaving when I'm feeling so comfortable after supper." Joe's parents talk with Joe some more. The three of them agree to try something new. They will make the switch on Monday mornings instead of Sunday nights. Soon, Joe's behavior on Sundays is better. Everyone enjoys the weekend more.

Joe's parents couldn't just let Joe misbehave. They were wise to try to find out what was wrong. This let Joe know his feelings matter. Changing the environment helped Joe choose better behavior.

Roles for Boys and Girls

A *role* is an expected behavior. Each culture tends to give different roles to boys and girls.

Over the years, our society's ideas about girls' and boys' roles have changed quite a bit. Even so, children still get messages from parents and other adults and from other children about what it means to be a boy or a girl.

At the end of a movie, 9-year-old Rhea said, "I cried when the boy fell out of the tree." Her mom said, "Me too. That was really sad."

After the same movie, 9-year-old Burton sniffled and wiped his eyes. His mom laughed at him. "Why are you crying?" she asked. "You're a big boy—and it's only a movie."

As parents, we don't want to let society's ideas about sex roles influence what we expect from our children. We need to be careful not to let these ideas excuse our children's misbehavior. Parents can expect boys and girls to help with cooking, laundry, or caring for younger children. They can teach both girls and boys that hitting is wrong and that crying is okay.

Ages and Stages

Children go through broad *developmental* stages. At different ages, we can expect certain skills and behaviors.

Grandma does not expect 7-year-old Jarek to do the laundry all alone. She does expect him to help her fold and put it away.

Dad does not expect 12-year-old Steven to go to bed at eight o'clock. He does expect him to understand the importance of getting enough sleep.

Each child also develops at his or her own rate.

Lucy, age 8, still believes in Santa Claus. Her friend Carlo, who is the same age, doesn't.

Mah Li and Jennie are best friends. They are 11. Mah Li doesn't see why Jennie wants to fix her hair and call boys all the time. She wishes Jennie still liked to play spy games and walk Jennie's little brother in the stroller.

Understanding stages helps parents know what they can expect. But it is also important *not* to let "it's a stage" *excuse* misbehavior—or *limit* expectations.

Greg, who is 11, and his friends are in the living room. They are playing a game and using bad language. Greg's mom knows that it is normal for children to learn and "try on" such words. Still, she tells her son and his friends, "Using bad words is rude. You're welcome to stay and play without that language. Still, if I hear more bad words, I'll know you've decided to go home."

Expect Your Child to Cooperate

Temperament, heredity, environment, sex roles, and ages and stages affect children's behavior. They are not the whole story. Children can act in a variety of ways.

Often, parents look at their children's negative behavior and simply shake their heads. They say:

- "His father is just like that."
- "She's a girl—she's sensitive."
- "She's ten? Watch out—the hormones are taking over!"
- "What else can you expect from a twelve-year-old boy?"

Some parents have come to accept misbehavior as "normal." We expect and accept it because we think we can do nothing about it:

Rafael doesn't like it when his little brother tags along to the basketball court. He lets his mother know it! "How come I always have to drag Felipe along?" Mom needs some quiet time to make phone calls and pay bills. But she gives in and keeps Felipe home. She tells herself, "I guess I can't expect a twelve-year-old to have time for a six-year-old."

Expectations are powerful. Children usually sense our expectations. When they do, they may try to live up (or down!) to them. This means that if we *expect* negative behavior, we may be *inviting* it. Doesn't it make sense, then, to expect cooperation?

Rafael's mom has a right to some quiet time. She can expect Rafael to understand this and cooperate. She also understands that Rafael needs a chance to be alone with his friends too. She might tell her son, "I need your help with Felipe tonight. Tomorrow night I'll keep him here with me."

Of course, expecting cooperation doesn't guarantee it. But over time, it does help your child grow more confident and responsible.

Expecting Cooperation

Think about a way to show your child that you expect cooperation. You might say something like this:

- "Please come help me fix supper. I'd like to hear more about your plans."
- "Look at Ernie's tail wagging! He knows you're about to take him for a walk."

Why Does My Child Misbehave?

You might be thinking, "Well, it helps to look at my parenting style. It's also nice to know what I can expect. But I still have a child who misbehaves! Why is that? What can I do about it?"

Wondering why your child misbehaves is normal. There is a reason behind most behavior.

Children Need to Belong

Children need to belong—to feel they are accepted. To do this, they may use positive behavior or misbehavior. Understanding how children seek to belong is important. Doing so will help you be a more effective parent.

Sometimes Children Belong by Misbehaving

Rudolf Dreikurs discovered that when children misbehave, they are *discouraged*. They want to belong, but they do not believe they can belong in useful ways. They find that misbehavior pays off. It helps them feel that they belong.

When children can't belong with positive behavior, they try to belong with four common misbehaviors. Dreikurs called these the four goals of misbehavior. Understanding these goals can help us know what children want when they misbehave. This can help us decide how to guide children to more positive behavior.

The Four Goals of Misbehavior

When children misbehave, they have a goal. They may feel the only way to belong is by:

- **attention**
- **power**
- **revenge**
- **display of inadequacy**

Attention

All children need *attention*. But some children seem to want attention all the time. If they believe they can't get attention in useful ways, then they seek it by misbehaving.

A misbehaving child is a discouraged child.
Rudolf Dreikurs

Children may look for attention when a parent is on the phone.

A child who misbehaves for attention will do something that is annoying to the parent. The parent steps in to correct the misbehavior. The child has gotten attention. All may be well for a short while. But it's not long before the child wants more attention.

Sometimes children ask for attention more quietly. A child might do nothing, expecting to be waited on. We call this *passive* misbehavior. It is still a bid for attention.

Some children choose to stage power struggles in public.

Power

Some children believe they belong only by being "the boss." These children seek the goal of *power*. A child who seeks power is telling the parent, "I am in control," "You can't make me!" or "You'd better do what I want!" The child might yell these things or fight out loud with the parent. Or the child might silently refuse to budge.

When a child seeks power, the parent feels angry. If the parent fights the child, the child fights back. If the parent gives in, the child has won the power struggle and so stops misbehaving.

Sometimes a child will do what the parent wants, but will do it extremely slowly or sloppily. This is a form of passive power. The child is saying, without words, "All right, I'll do it—just to get you off my back. But I'll do it *my* way. You can't make me do it *your* way."

Revenge

Some children want to be the boss but can't win in a power struggle with their parents. These children decide that the way to belong is to get even. Dreikurs called this goal *revenge*. A child who wants revenge may say or do something hurtful. Or the child may stare

A child who wants revenge will try to hurt the parent.

angrily at the parent. Either way, the parent feels hurt and angry and tries to get even. The result is often a growing "war" of revenge. Both the child and the parent have angry, hurt feelings.

Displaying Inadequacy

Some children just give up. For them, the way to belong is to get others to leave them alone. Their behavior says, "I can't do it." Dreikurs called this *displaying inadequacy*. When a child gives up, the parent feels like giving up too. When this happens, the child's goal has been met. The parent has agreed to expect nothing from the child.

For most children, this helplessness is not total. It usually happens in certain areas of the child's life. This might be in schoolwork, sports, or other social activities. It can be in any area where the child feels unable to succeed.

Children don't know that their misbehavior has a goal. Children may also use the same behavior to seek different goals. Be aware that parents don't cause children's misbehavior. By our own behavior, though, we may reinforce it. The key to knowing the goal is to look at the three clues: how you feel, what you do, and how your child responds.

Children who display inadequacy have given up. Often, their parents have too.

How Can I Build a Better Relationship With My Child?

One way to help children belong is to focus on building positive relationships with them. Strong positive relationships can go a long way toward helping children learn to cooperate and be responsible. Four ingredients of strong relationships are:

- showing respect
- having fun
- giving encouragement
- showing love

Showing Respect

Parents often complain that their children do not respect them. Yet, many times, adults show children a lack of respect. How? By nagging, yelling, hitting, or talking down. By doing things for children that they can do for themselves. By following a double standard.

Everyone Deserves Respect

In a democratic family, no one is considered more or less important than anyone else. You show your respect when you treat your child like an equal.

- Does this mean that you are both the same? No. You know more and have more life experience than your child. You have more responsibilities. But both you and your child are human beings. You both deserve respect.
- Does it mean that your child can tell you what to do? Or that you are not in charge? No. You need to be in charge. It is your job to guide your child. But you can guide your child respectfully.

A good rule to remember is that you want to treat your child with the same respect you would show a friend. It may take some time for your child to begin to show respect back to you. Don't give up if this doesn't happen right away. We all need to practice this habit and be willing to take the first step.

Having Fun

Who doesn't want to have fun? Fun is a key part of our relationships with friends. What about our family relationships? Having fun with our children can be simple.

Identifying the Goal

Look at three things:

- **how you feel when the misbehavior happens**

- **what you do about the misbehavior**

- **how your child responds to what you do**

In Chapter 2, we will look more closely at the goals of misbehavior and what to do when your child misbehaves.

Start by Smiling

Where to begin? A good-morning smile can set the tone for your child's whole day—and for yours. Take a step back and laugh at yourself. When you see humor in your own problems, children can see it in theirs. When you laugh at your mistakes, children see that mistakes are okay.

Keep It Simple

Having fun doesn't have to be a big project. Even the busiest of families can add fun to their daily lives.

Chores like fixing meals or shopping for groceries become times to enjoy or even be a little silly. On the bus or in the car, you can play word games. Have your children read jokes to you. Watch a funny TV show while you fold laundry together.

Children love to laugh. They love to see the funny side of things. For all of us, a few minutes of humor are worth several hours of conflict!

Plan Time for Fun

Planning time for fun is also a good idea. If possible, spend at least a short time each day with your child. Let the child lead the way. Your child might want to play a game, toss a ball back and forth, or work on a project. Bedtime offers a chance for you and your child to share some one-on-one time.

When you start having fun with children, you may be surprised by the results. You may notice your children having more fun (and fighting less) with sisters, brothers, and friends. You will find being a parent more enjoyable.

Giving Encouragement

We must believe in our children if they are to believe in themselves:

- To feel capable and loved, children need lots of encouragement.
- To be ready to truly cooperate, children need to feel good about themselves.

Notice What Is Special

Every child is unique. Your child has many special and wonderful qualities. When you notice these qualities and point them out, your child will feel *encouraged*. With each bit of encouragement, children grow to like themselves a little bit better and feel more confident.

For Your *Family*

This activity won't take long. Do it when your family is together—perhaps at suppertime.

- Take turns telling about something good that happened to each of you during the day.

- At first, you might want to start the conversation. Or, ask one of your children: "What is something nice that happened to you today? Tell us about it."

- If a child says nothing good happened, ask, "What's something nice you did for someone else?"

Do this family sharing as often as you can.

Encouragement STEP

Start to notice when you say no to your child. Say no as little as possible:

- **Stop yourself <u>before</u> saying "Why do you always do this?" or "Cut it out—I mean it!"**

- **If you can't think of a positive response, say nothing.**

- **Change the subject or perhaps move to another room.**

Look for chances to turn no into yes. This will encourage your child:

- **"Yes, you may have one cookie."**

- **"Yes, you've played your horn for fifteen minutes. You're halfway done practicing."**

Chapter 3 deals with encouragement. Each chapter of this book has an "Encouragement Step" to help you get in the encouragement habit. Throughout the book, you'll also find short activities that let you focus on yourself—because you need encouragement too!

Notice Your Child's Efforts

Encouragement means giving less importance to children's mistakes and more importance to their strengths. It focuses on efforts. It tells children, "I have confidence in you."

You don't have to wait for your child to finish a whole assignment before commenting on the effort the child is making. Each step toward finishing a job is part of the effort. Each step deserves encouragement. When you notice the steps along the way, you help your child keep going.

Teach Your Child to Help Others

Encourage your child to help others. Caring about others comes more easily when we first love and care about ourselves.

Showing Love

To feel secure, each child must have at least one adult to love and to be loved by. You show love by your words and by your actions:

- by saying "I love you"
- by giving hugs and pats on the back
- by speaking and acting with respect
- by allowing your child to grow in responsibility and independence

You Have Taken the First Big Step

In Chapter 1, you have learned many things about yourself and your child:

- You have seen the importance of setting limits and giving choices.
- You have learned about the goals of misbehavior.
- You have thought about your expectations.
- You have learned that you can expect your child to cooperate.
- You have learned that your child wants to belong.
- You have looked at ways to show respect, encouragement, and love for your child.
- You have remembered how important it is to have fun together.

In doing these things, you have taken an important step in meeting your parenting goals.

THIS WEEK

When your children misbehave, watch them *and* yourself. Decide what the goal is. Ask yourself:

1. What did my child do?

2. How did I feel?

3. What did I do about it?

4. What did my child do then?

5. What is the goal of misbehavior?

6. What is one way I could encourage a more positive goal?

JUST FOR YOU

Stress

Being a parent is a stressful job! You can ease and handle the stress in many ways, including:

- **Deep breathing.** Breathe deeply for about fifteen seconds. Let your breathing pace itself—don't force it. Quietly say "calm" as you breathe in, and say "down" as you breathe out. Do this until you feel relaxed.

- **Progresssive relaxation.** This reduces stress and creates a pleasant emotional state. Begin by tensing your hands into fists, then relaxing them. Learn how muscle tension feels so you can relax a tense feeling.

- **Accept yourself.** Every day, accept yourself and take time to concentrate on your positive qualities. Make self-affirming statements, like "I'm learning to become more effective," or "I'm growing more confident."

POINTS TO REMEMBER

1. The challenge of parenting is to raise a child who is happy, healthy, confident, cooperative, loving and lovable, and responsible.

2. You can help your child to cooperate and be responsible by setting limits and giving choices.

3. Temperament, heredity, environment, ages and stages, and sex roles all affect your child's behavior.

4. Expectations are powerful. If you expect misbehavior, your child will probably misbehave. If you expect cooperation, your child will be more likely to cooperate.

5. All children want to belong. They get a feeling of belonging through both useful behavior and misbehavior.

6. There are four goals of misbehavior:
   - attention
   - power
   - revenge
   - display of inadequacy

7. You can build a good relationship with your child by:
   - showing respect
   - having fun
   - giving encouragement
   - showing love

Chart 1
IDENTIFYING THE FOUR GOALS OF MISBEHAVIOR

How do you feel?	What do you usually do?	How does your child usually respond?	Goal
Bothered, annoyed	Remind, nag, scold	Stops temporarily. Later, misbehaves again	Attention
Angry, threatened	Punish, fight back, or give in	Continues to misbehave, defies you, or does what you've asked slowly or sloppily	Power
Angry, extremely hurt	Get back at child, punish	Misbehaves even more, keeps trying to get even	Revenge
Hopeless, like giving up	Give up, agree that child is helpless	Does not respond or improve	Display of Inadequacy

Understanding **Beliefs** *and* **Feelings**

You've learned that your child needs to belong. Misbehavior is one way your child seeks to do this. This does not mean that your child consciously thinks, "I want power" or "I want to get even." Rather, children discover that misbehavior works for them—it gives them a payoff. They know this by how parents respond.

What Can I Do When My Child Misbehaves?

Do parents cause children to misbehave? No. Our children choose the way they behave. We may reinforce the misbehavior by responding the way our children expect. By changing our responses by doing the unexpected, our children won't reach their negative goals.

If we respond as our children expect us to, they are on the way to reaching their negative goals. Our responses help them get there.

But if we respond differently, we can send a completely different message. We can let them know by our words and actions that we choose not to support their misbehavior. In this way, over time, we can help them choose positive goals and positive behavior.

This won't happen overnight. This whole book is about how we can support our children's positive goals. But we must start someplace. A good place to begin is by doing the unexpected.

Here's what you will learn . . .

- **The way to improve a child's behavior is to change your approach.**

- **Your child has beliefs about how to belong.**

- **Your child's feelings and actions come from these beliefs.**

- **You have feelings and beliefs too.**

- **You can change your feelings and beliefs so that you can help your child.**

Do the Unexpected

When you do the unexpected, you do the opposite of what a child expects. This way, the child won't get the usual payoff. Your response won't support the misbehavior. Then, the child may need to find a more useful way to belong. Let's look at some examples.

Attention

Joe wants his dad to play a game. But Dad has to make a phone call. So Joe plays with his brother Richie. He pounds the pegs as he moves them across the board. Dad says, "Play quieter, Joe." "Okay," Joe answers. After a few minutes, Joe starts to slap the cards down as he deals. Dad sighs. "Joe," he says, "I asked you to play quietly." Two minutes later, Joe whines, "Dad—Richie's cheating!"

Clues to Joe's Goal

1.　Dad feels *annoyed*.

2.　Dad gives attention: He *nags* and *reminds* Joe to cooperate.

3.　Joe *stops misbehaving for a while*. Later, he *does something else to get Dad's attention*.

Dad knows that Joe wants *attention*.

What Else Could Dad Do?
- He could ignore Joe's whining and noise. If Dad does this, he needs to keep his face and body language calm.
- He could give Joe a choice. He could say, "Joe, I need to talk on the phone. You may play quietly or take the game to another room. You decide."
- If Joe is willing to cooperate, Dad could play the game with him later.

At another time, Dad can give Joe attention when he is not asking for it.

Power

"Can Marie stay over Saturday night?" asks Saundra, age 11. "No," Mom reminds her, "because this is your weekend to visit your dad." Saundra starts trying to get Mom to call him to change the weekend. "That's between you and your dad," Mom says, starting to feel angry. Saundra gets angry too, and she and her mom argue. Finally, Mom shouts, "Oh, all right. I'll call your dad and explain."

What Is Misbehavior?

- **actions or words that are disrespectful or ignore others' rights**

- **refusal to cooperate when the child knows how to cooperate**

- **behavior that is dangerous to the child or others**

Clues to Saundra's Goal

1. Mom feels *angry.*

2. Mom *fights with Saundra.*

3. Saundra *fights back,* and Mom gives in.

Mom knows that Saundra wants to *be the boss.* Saundra's goal is *power.*

What Else Could Mom Do?

- She could refuse either to fight or to give in by remaining silent or leaving the room when Saundra tries to force Mom into making Saundra's call for her.

- At another time, when Mom is not angry, she could explain to Saundra that it's her responsibility to discuss any plan changes with her dad.

Revenge

Cindy's class is going on an end-of-school trip to an amusement park. A week before the trip, Cindy sees that she hasn't saved enough money. She takes ten dollars from her dad's wallet. That night, her dad notices that he is short ten dollars. He finds the money on the table by Cindy's bed. Dad is shocked and hurt. He yells at Cindy, "You little thief! I'll teach you to steal from me!" Cindy cries, "You had no right to go snooping in my stuff. That money was mine!" Dad shouts, "You can just stay in school on the day of the field trip!" "I hate you!" Cindy yells back.

Clues to Cindy's Goal

1. Dad feels *hurt.* He *wants to get back* at Cindy.

2. Dad *tries to hurt Cindy* by taking away the trip and calling her a thief.

3. Cindy *hurts Dad back* by telling her dad she hates him.

Dad knows that Cindy's goal is to *get revenge.*

What Else Could Dad Do?

- Dad can *refuse to feel hurt* and *not say anything else that is hurtful.*
- He could *refuse to fight.*
- He could *talk to Cindy* when they are both calm. He could say, "Cindy, I have a problem. I see my ten dollars on your night table. Help me understand what's going on."

Changing a cycle of revenge takes time. But Cindy can't have a battle of revenge if Dad won't join in. This will give both Dad and Cindy a chance to cool down and think. Dad also needs to look for ways to build trust and respect.

Display of Inadequacy

For winter term, Shawn's fourth-grade class is playing basketball in gym twice a week. Shawn tells his mom, "Nobody wants me on their team. I can't shoot good. And I can't hold onto the ball." Mom has tried to help Shawn practice. She shoots hoops with him. She asks his older brother to help too. If Shawn misses the hoop once or loses the ball, he says, "I'll never be any good at this." Mom doesn't know how else to help. She says, "Maybe basketball isn't your game, Shawn. I'll talk to the gym teacher. You don't have to play if you don't want to."

Clues to Shawn's Goal

1. Mom feels *hopeless*. After doing what she can to help, she *wants to give up* on Shawn's playing basketball.
2. Mom *gives up*. She tells Shawn that she agrees he can't play basketball.
3. Shawn has Mom's permission to fail. He is *not likely to improve* at basketball.

Shawn has said, "I can't," and Mom has agreed. Mom knows that Shawn's goal is to *display inadequacy*.

What Else Could Mom Do?

- She could *refuse to give up on Shawn*. She might say, "I know you can learn to shoot and dribble. That's why you are playing basketball in school—so you can learn it."
- She could be careful *not to pity Shawn*. If Shawn thinks Mom feels sorry for him, he'll feel sorry for himself too.
- She could *encourage Shawn* as he learns to play basketball. He might tell her he made one basket but missed all the others. She can say, "So you see, you *can* make a basket! You are learning!"
- She could *encourage Shawn in other ways*. When Shawn figures out a math problem, Mom might say, "I knew you'd get it if you stuck to it."

Sometimes a child who says "I can't" wants to have attention, not to give up. How can you tell the difference? The attention seeker wants parents to busy themselves with the child. The child who gives up wants to be left alone. If your child says "I can't," use your feelings as a guide. Do you feel annoyed? If so, you can guess the child's goal is attention. Do you feel like giving up? If you do, the goal is probably to display inadequacy.

A child who gives up is *extremely discouraged*. Using lots of support and encouragement with a child who gives up is important. In Chapter 3 you will learn more about how to encourage your child.

It's Worth the Effort

Doing the unexpected is not always easy. It means looking hard at how you feel. You also have to change your view so you can respond in a different way. Making this effort is important. Our reactions affect how children grow and learn. Knowing this makes the effort worthwhile.

Why Do Children Become Discouraged?

You have seen that children who misbehave are discouraged. Why do children become discouraged? Two things that affect how children decide to belong are beliefs and feelings.

Children Have Beliefs

Children have *beliefs* about how they need to belong. We call beliefs that lead to misbehavior "faulty."

Children's Faulty Beliefs

- **Attention:** "I belong only by being noticed—even if that makes problems for Dad or Mom."
- **Power:** "I belong only by being the boss—even if that leads to a fight. If I can get Mom or Dad to fight with me, I have power."
- **Revenge:** "I am not lovable. I belong only by hurting Dad or Mom. I want them to feel as hurt as I do."
- **Display of Inadequacy:** "I belong by convincing Mom or Dad that I can't do things. In fact, when I try to do something and fail, I *don't* belong."

Each of the beliefs of the goals of misbehavior has a flip side—a positive belief that can lead to better behavior.

The Flip Side: Positive Beliefs

- **Involvement:** "I want to be a part of things. Please help me learn to contribute."
- **Independence:** "I want to be independent. Please give me choices so I can learn to be responsible."
- **Fairness:** "I want things to be fair. Please help me learn to cooperate."
- **Being competent:** "I need time to think by myself. I want to succeed. Please help me learn to trust myself."

Knowing the flip side of the four goals helps. We can use this information to help our children move:

- from attention to involvement
- from power to independence
- from revenge to being fair
- from displaying inadequacy to being thoughtful and competent

We want to do even more than this. We want to encourage our children to seek all of the positive goals and help our children develop *all* of the positive beliefs.

Encourage the Positive

Help your child change faulty beliefs into positive beliefs. How?

By helping children take part. Encourage children to help with family projects. Show them how to cooperate with other people. In this way, they can be a part of things and can be helpful to others too.

By giving choices. Give your child choices. Let your child live with the choice. When possible, let your child do things alone. In this way, your child will grow more confident. Your child will begin to make better choices.

By being fair. Guide your child to play and share equally. Treat your child fairly and with respect so your child will trust you. In this way, your child will see that people can be fair and trustworthy. When this is true, there is no need to get even.

Every misbehavior has a "flip side."

Sometimes you will try to be fair, but your child will think you aren't fair enough. If this happens, check your feelings. Your child may be seeking power or revenge. Don't join in the power struggle. Keep being as fair as you can.

By noticing and teaching courage. Teach your child to try things and to keep trying. Encourage your child to use words to explain worries or to talk about problems. Notice your child's strengths. In these ways, your child learns courage.

Where Do Beliefs Come From?

We formed some of our most basic beliefs when we were very young. These beliefs were not always logical. Still, they made sense to us. Many of these beliefs remain with us today. We are not even aware of some of them. Sometimes they can cause us problems.

Just like ours, our children's beliefs come from experiences they had when they were very young. They come from each child's view of four things:

- what is important in the family
- the child's place in the family
- what the parents say and do
- the style of parenting

What Is Important in the Family

Every family has a unique mood or tone. We call this the *family atmosphere*. Also, adults in every family have *values*. The combination of atmosphere and values gives the child a message about what is important in a family.

Children Can Tell What Is Important
The parents set the stage for how children view what is important. Children usually know, for example, if music or sports are important to a parent. This is because the parent will enjoy these activities and will often teach them to the child.

Some values may not be stated but are still obvious to a child.

A child sees that parents talk about problems together. The child learns to value cooperation.

A child sees that parents argue and refuse to compromise. The child learns that fighting and getting one's own way are how to solve problems.

Thinking About Beliefs

Notice your child's positive behavior. Think about the belief behind this good behavior.

Also notice your child's misbehavior. Think about the belief here too. Think of one way to encourage the "flip side" of the belief.

- "I believe telling the truth is important. When we do, we learn to trust each other."
- "I believe saying please and thank you shows respect."
- "I believe talking, not hitting, is the way to solve problems. Hitting hurts."

When you share a value, be ready to listen to your child's point of view too.

Act as You'd Like Your Child to Act

Your child will learn more from what you do than from what you say. Children watch your behavior and attitude. Then they choose for themselves the qualities they value and want. The process of choosing takes time.

At times, you'll be disappointed when it seems that your child is learning negative values. When you see this happening, think carefully about what your child might be learning from your actions.

John saw that his daughter Jasmine often insisted on having her own way. John felt worried. He thought hard about how to help her learn to cooperate better. He realized that his tone with her was often bossy. Especially after work, when he was tired, John sometimes ordered Jasmine around rather than being friendly. John decided to change how he acted toward Jasmine. It was hard at first, but it got easier. After a while, Jasmine's bossiness happened less often.

It is important for parents to do as they say.

- If we tell our children not to lie, we tell the truth to them— and to others too.
- If we tell our children to be polite, we treat them and others courteously.
- If we tell our children not to hit, we do not hit.

Parenting Styles

In Chapter 1 you read about parenting styles. The parenting style leads children to certain beliefs.

- **When parents give orders, some children see a need to fight and compete. Some come to believe that being the boss is the way to belong.**
- **When parents give in, many children come to believe that no one's wishes but theirs matter.**

Saying and Doing

Think about a value you want to teach your child. Some examples of values are honesty, education, generosity, good manners, or music.

- **What can you <u>say</u> to teach your child the value?**

- **What can you <u>do</u> to show your child that the value is truly important?**

- When parents give choices, children learn that cooperation is a way people can live together. They are likely to believe that every person is important.

We Had Parents Too

The way our parents raised us affects our present approach to parenting.

- We may have been brought up to believe we must be the best at anything we do. So we may push our children. We may want others to think our children are the smartest, or the most talented, or the strongest.

- Maybe we were brought up to believe that we deserve to have our own way. So we may try to force our children to do exactly what we want. Or we may expect other people to do as our children wish.

- We may have been brought up to respect others. Then we will probably expect other people to do the same. We'll teach our children to show respect to us, to themselves, and to other people.

Where Do Feelings Come From?

Through their beliefs, children make choices about how to belong. Feelings also affect how children decide to belong.

Everybody has feelings. Adults have them. Children have them too. Where do feelings come from? Why do we feel happy, angry, or sad?

We often think of feelings as magical things we can't control. We say: "He made me so angry!" Or, "She's going to drive me crazy!"

Feelings Come From Beliefs

Here is something to think about: Each of us creates our own feelings. Many people find this surprising. Yet it is true.

- **If we believe people are friendly and can be trusted, we create good feelings. We do this to bring ourselves closer to other people.**

- **If we believe people are unfriendly and can't be trusted, we create negative feelings. We do this to keep people away.**

Think about your child at the age of 4 or 5. Did your child ever get so excited that you would say the child "lost control"?

Everything can also be different.

Alfred Adler

Bonita was going to have a party for her fourth birthday. She was excited. During the party, she became sillier and sillier.

Five-year-old Randy's grandmother was coming to visit. He grew more and more wild and excited as he waited for her to arrive.

Young children *do* seem to "lose control" of their feelings at times. Anyone who has seen a temper tantrum knows what that means! As parents, part of our job is to help our children learn to take responsibility for their feelings.

Children's Feelings Have a Purpose

Some children believe they can belong by cooperating. Then the children create good feelings toward others. The good feelings help them reach their goal of belonging.

When children believe they must misbehave to belong, they create negative feelings.

Aparna's dad is studying. Aparna bumps her head on the table. It doesn't really hurt. But Aparna starts to cry. Dad stops studying. He asks, "Did you hurt yourself?" "Yes," sniffles Aparna. "Will you read with me, Dad?"

Dad needs to study. But he feels guilty about not spending more time with his daughter. He thinks for a minute. Then he says, "I'm sorry, but I can't read with you now. I have to study." Aparna starts to cry harder. "But I hurt my head," she sobs. "I think it will be okay," Dad says. Aparna keeps crying. Dad ignores her.

Later, at supper, Aparna is happier. Dad says to her, "Let's clean up the dishes and read a chapter in your book."

Aparna wants attention. Dad is helping her see that crying isn't a good way to get it.

Crying can also be a way to display inadequacy. Or it can be a way to get power or revenge.

Eric had a habit of waiting until the last minute to do his homework. His mom would watch him put off his work. She would feel worried and say, "Eric, you need to get started on your paper." Eric would say, "Quit nagging. I'll do it."

Finally, Eric would start his work. Soon he would come to his mom. "This isn't fair," he'd tell her. "The teacher gave me way too much work. You need to help me." Mom would feel angry. "I told you to get started sooner!" she would say. Then Eric would start to cry and yell. "You've got to help me!" he'd shout. "Or else the stupid teacher will flunk me! And it'll be your fault!"

By then, Mom's heart would be pounding. She wanted to yell back. She wanted to tell Eric he was being a brat.

CHAPTER TWO   35

Eric had his mom hooked in a battle for power and revenge. He wanted to have things his way. He wanted Mom to feel guilty. What could Mom do? She could refuse to join the battle. Instead of nagging, she could keep quiet. Instead of yelling or calling Eric a name, she could ignore his tantrum.

Doing this might be hard at first. Eric needs to see that crying and yelling won't make his mom feel mad or guilty. They won't make school any more "fair."

Of course, not all negative feelings are a sign of misbehavior.

A child's friend might say something mean. The child might feel hurt and cry.

A child might work hard on a paper at the school computer. Then something happens so the file is erased. The child might feel angry.

These sad and angry feelings are natural. Parents can listen and show that they care. In Chapter 4, you will learn more about listening for feelings. For now, check to see if your child is using feelings as a way to misbehave. Look at:

- **how you feel**
- **what you do**
- **how your child responds to what you do**

This will help you decide what to do. If your child is misbehaving, don't "buy into" the feelings.

Parents' Feelings Have a Purpose Too

When our children misbehave, we may become annoyed or angry. Our feelings have a purpose: to control our children.

You have seen that controlling children—giving orders—does not help them learn to cooperate or be responsible. Once you decide to set limits and give choices, you won't need to feel annoyed or angry. Instead, you can change your feelings to fit your parenting goal. In doing so, you may be able to influence your child to find a better way to belong.

How Can I Help My Child and Myself?

You know that parents don't *cause* children to misbehave. We do play a part in keeping misbehavior going. We do this by responding in ways children expect us to. Can we make children behave? Can we change their beliefs and feelings?

Really, the only person you can change is you! You can change how you respond to your child's misbehavior. When you do this, you help your child. How? You don't give the payoff your child expects. You don't support the misbehavior. This means your child will have to find a new way to belong.

Change Your Response

Take three steps to change your response to your child.

1. **Decide to change.**
2. **Change your purpose.**
3. **Change your beliefs and feelings.**

Decide to Change

First, look hard at the way you respond when your child misbehaves. Decide to change what needs changing. Tell yourself: "When my child sees how I let misbehavior upset me, I am not helping my child. I'm cooperating with the misbehavior. That doesn't make sense. I will have to change how I respond."

Change Your Purpose

Look hard at what *your* purpose is when your child misbehaves. Ask yourself:

- Do I want to give attention? Or help my child be self-reliant?
- Do I want to show who's the boss? Or help my child be independent and responsible?
- Do I want to get even? Or show that I understand?
- Do I want to let my child off the hook? Or help my child be self-confident?

When your child misbehaves, think about the purpose of your reaction before you do anything else.

Change Your Beliefs and Feelings

Check what you believe and what you are feeling. To do this, look at your "self-talk"—at what you are telling yourself.

Many parents get into a habit of a certain kind of self-talk. It's called *demanding, can't standing, complaining,* and *blaming.*

- **Demanding:** We demand that things be different. We tell ourselves, "My children should not do that. They should do this instead."
- **Can't Standing:** We tell ourselves that we just can't stand for our children to misbehave.
- **Complaining:** We complain to ourselves, "This is awful. This is terrible."
- **Blaming:** We blame the child or ourselves and think, "My child is disappointing. I'm a bad parent."

You can change your self-talk. To do this, start by looking at your feelings. Ask yourself: "Am I annoyed? angry? hurt? discouraged? Or am I *committed* to helping my child stop misbehaving?"

You don't need to feel angry with your child. You can talk yourself into feeling calm and capable of changing your response.

Marissa, 10 years old, was mad at her father. "You don't care about me!" she yelled. "You buy yourself nice clothes for work! But you won't buy me anything I want!" Dad felt angry and hurt. He wanted to get back at Marissa. But Dad stopped himself and kept quiet.

He thought about what he was saying to himself. It went something like this: "How dare she talk to me this way? She'd better stop it! Why is she such a brat? I'm a bad father."

Then Dad asked himself, "What do I want to do here? Do I want to get even? No, I want to help Marissa cooperate. Do I need to feel hurt and angry? No, it would be better to try to understand why she is acting like this. I don't like to be talked to that way, but I can handle it. I would like her to be more respectful, but she isn't right now. She's misbehaving, but she isn't a bad kid. I'm not a bad father."

Dad changed his self-talk. Now he was in a much better position to act. Dad might do many things next:

- He could say, "Marissa, you're really angry with me. Do you want to talk about it?"
- He could say, "I don't like being talked to that way. I'll be glad to discuss this with you when you can be respectful."
- He could ignore it for the moment and discuss the problem later.

When you change your self-talk, you aren't playing some kind of word game. You are working to find a new purpose, feeling, and belief. *You stop helping your child misbehave.* You also do it so you can start helping your child find a better way to belong.

Changing Your Self-Talk

When you are upset with your child, ask yourself:

- **What am I telling myself?**
- **What can I tell myself instead?**

The more you do this, the more prepared you will be to respond to misbehavior.

Help Yourself Out

It isn't easy to change your response to misbehavior. It is worth the effort. You can use these ideas to help yourself out.

Listen to your tone of voice. Sometimes we say the right thing, but it comes out too harsh. Or the way we say it tells the child we don't really mean it. Listen to how your voice sounds. If you need to, take a deep breath. Speak calmly and respectfully.

Watch your body language. This is another way to check yourself. Are you leaning in too close to your child? Does your body feel tense? Again, take a deep breath and relax your body.

Do the unexpected. You learned how to do the unexpected earlier in this chapter. When you do the unexpected, your child doesn't get the "payoff" he or she wants.

We all have times when we just need to get away and calm down.

Distract yourself. When your feelings are strong, think about something else. You might think ahead to a visit you will have with a friend. You could think back to a good time you've had with your child. Plan a shopping list. If you need to, leave the room and do something that will calm you down. Fold laundry. Walk around the block. Look at a magazine.

Encouragement
STEP

Dealing with misbehavior is challenging. It is also an opportunity. It gives you a chance to see your child in new ways.

Look for ways to see the "flip side" of your child's behavior. Here are examples:

- **A child who seems bossy may also be a leader.**

- **A child who wants things to be fair may see many different points of view.**

Use your sense of humor. A sense of humor can help both you and your child. You might say, "Yes, I do lie awake at night plotting ways to torture you!" Or, "No, I never was a kid. Can't you tell?"

Use humor like this carefully. You don't want your child to think you are being sarcastic. You can also laugh at your own mistakes. This helps your child see that you know you aren't perfect. And it can help *you* change your self-talk.

Don't feel guilty. Guilt feelings won't help you. Deciding to change will. If you've yelled and now feel bad about it, tell yourself, "I'm sorry I yelled. Next time, I won't do that." Then let it go. No one is perfect—we all make mistakes. You know that a child who misbehaves is not bad. A parent who goofs isn't a bad parent, either!

You Have Taken Another Big Step

In Chapter 2, you have learned more about your child and yourself. You also have learned and started to practice parenting skills.

- You have seen that misbehaving is a way for children to belong.
- You have begun to think about what to do when your child misbehaves.
- You have learned about ways children form their beliefs and feelings.
- You have seen that the way to help your child change is to change yourself.
- You have discovered that you can change your beliefs and feelings.

For Your *Family*

Notice when your child helps out, cooperates, or takes responsibility. Let your child know you have noticed. Use the words "I appreciate":

- **"I appreciate when you put the trash out without being told. Thank you."**
- **"I appreciated how you chatted with my boss while he waited for me to come to the phone."**

Encourage everyone in your family to notice and appreciate when others help.

THIS WEEK

Keep paying attention to the goals of misbehavior. When your children misbehave, watch them and yourself. Decide what the goal is. Ask yourself:

1. What did my child do?
2. How did I feel?
3. What did I do about it?
4. What did my child do then?
5. What do I think the goal of misbehavior was?
6. What are *two or three ways* I could encourage a more positive goal?

JUST FOR YOU

Fighting Your Irrational Beliefs

Beliefs cause emotions. If you choose to think of unpleasant events, you will have unpleasant feelings. How you feel results from your thoughts. Your irrational beliefs cause problems and interfere with your happiness. They take the form of demanding, complaining, and blaming.

Your discouraging words and self-talk reflect your beliefs. When you believe absolute words such as *I should, I must,* or *I have to,* you place conditions on yourself.

Learn to think rationally:

- Choose new thoughts.
- Learn to look at negative situations in a logical way.
- Look at your wants as preferences, not "musts."
- See your "catastrophes" as the simple disappointments or inconveniences they are.

Ask yourself these questions to help fight irrational beliefs:

1. What am I thinking? Am I demanding or blaming?
2. Is my belief rational or irrational? How do I know this?
3. What are the consequences of continuing these beliefs?
4. What are the consequences of changing my beliefs?

POINTS TO REMEMBER

1. To identify a child's goal, look at:
   - how you feel when the misbehavior happens
   - what you do about the misbehavior
   - how the child responds to what you do

2. The only behavior you can change is your own. To help a child stop misbehaving, concentrate on changing how you respond. Do or say something your child does not expect.

3. Beliefs and feelings affect how a child decides to belong.

4. To help your child form positive beliefs, you can:
   - Help your child take part.
   - Give choices.
   - Be fair.
   - Notice and teach courage.

5. Beliefs come from a child's view of what is important in the family, the child's place, what parents say and do, and the style of parenting.

6. Feelings come from beliefs. You can change your beliefs and feelings by changing your self-talk. This can help you respond to misbehavior in a way that helps your child.

Chart 2
DEALING WITH MISBEHAVIOR

Remember, to decide your child's goal, look at:

1. how you feel when the misbehavior happens
2. what you do about the misbehavior
3. how your child responds to what you do

Goal	Examples of misbehavior	What parents can do:	Ways to encourage positive goals and beliefs:
Attention	**Active:** Interrupting, clowning **Passive:** Forgetting, not doing chores, expecting to be waited on	Don't give attention on demand. Ignore when possible. Don't wait on child. Give attention for good behavior at other times.	Say thank you when child helps. Notice when child contributes.
Power	**Active:** Throwing tantrums, making demands, arguing **Passive:** Being stubborn, doing what parent wants slowly or sloppily	Refuse to fight or give in. Withdraw from power contest. If possible, leave room. Let consequence occur for child.	Give choices. Let child make decisions. Ask for help, cooperation at other times.
Revenge	**Active:** Being rude, saying hurtful things, being violent **Passive:** Giving hurtful looks, hurtfully refusing to cooperate	Refuse to feel hurt or angry. Don't hurt child back. At other times, work to build trust. Help child feel loved.	Be as fair as you can. Say thank you when child helps. Notice and appreciate when child contributes.
Display of Inadequacy	**Passive only:** Quitting easily, not trying	Do not pity. Stop all criticizing. Notice all efforts, no matter how small. Don't give up on child.	Focus on child's strengths, talents. Notice when child makes wise choices. Notice when child thinks of others. Give lots of encouragement.

CHAPTER THREE

Encouraging
Your Child *and* Yourself

You want your child to form positive beliefs, to find positive ways to belong. Doing this will be easier for any child if the child has strong *self-esteem*. In fact, self-esteem is important for all of us—children and adults alike.

What Is Self-Esteem?
It is a belief that we belong and are

- accepted
- strong and capable
- loved

Self-esteem helps our children know that they belong, can contribute, and are loved. It helps them create successes. It helps them get through problems. It helps them say "I can" and "I will."

You Can Help Build Your Child's Self-Esteem

When parents believe in children, they help children believe in themselves. When parents show their children respect, they help children respect themselves and others.

Show that you believe in and respect your child. There are many ways to do this. One of the best is by being *encouraging*.

Here's what you will learn . . .

- **You can use encouragement to help build your child's self-esteem.**
- **Encouragement can help your child to feel loved, accepted, respected, and valued.**
- **Praise and encouragement are not the same thing.**
- **You also need to encourage yourself.**

What Is Encouragement?

Encouragement is a skill to help children grow in self-esteem. It is a way to show children that they belong and are

- accepted
- capable
- loved

Look at the words *encourage* and *discourage*. They both include the word *courage*. Courage is an important part of self-esteem. It means a willingness to make an effort.

An encouraged child has strong self-esteem. This child has the courage to cooperate, to try new things, and to be responsible.

A discouraged child has little self-esteem and won't make an effort. This child doesn't have the courage to choose positive ways to belong.

Jonah's younger sister Ruthie asks for help making a poster for school. As he helps Ruthie, Jonah keeps going to his mom. He waves things in front of her and says, "Look at this guy I drew for Ruthie." "Do you like how I cut this out for Ruthie?" "Mom, where's the double-sided tape?" Jonah wants to help his sister, but he is not sure of himself. His self-esteem needs to be stronger.

Jonah's mom can encourage him by ignoring his attention seeking. Later she can look for ways to give Jonah attention when he isn't seeking it.

How Can I Encourage My Child?

Like Jonah's mom, you want to help your child. You won't do this by reinforcing misbehavior or criticizing. Encouragement starts with showing respect.

You know that everyone deserves respect. Respect for yourself and respect for others go hand in hand. This is true for children and for adults.

Justin, age 10, is building a model rocket. He has worked on it a long time. It's almost done. Justin's dad is looking for a new job. Today, Dad gets a phone call. He learns that someone else got the job he had wanted. Dad hangs up the phone and sighs. Justin is putting his model away. He moves too fast and drops the rocket. Parts fly everywhere. Justin shouts and starts to cry. His dad says to him, "This has been a bad afternoon for both of us. I feel frustrated. And I can tell you do too."

For Dad, not getting a job is more important than a broken model. But Dad has shown that he knows Justin's problems are important too. Dad didn't put himself down for not getting the job. He didn't put Justin down for being careless or for crying. Dad has shown respect for himself and for his son. If Dad keeps doing this, Justin is likely to learn to respect himself and others too.

When your child receives your respect, the child feels valued. Seeing that you respect yourself, your child sees a model of self-esteem. This is encouraging to your child.

Encouragement is based on the idea of respect. Like respect, it is something children need all the time. You can learn to get in the "encouragement habit." Learn and practice some skills to show that you:

- Love and accept your child.

- Notice when your child tries or improves.

- Appreciate your child.

- Have faith in your child.

Let's take a closer look at each way to encourage.

Love and Accept Your Child

Every child is special. Like each of us, every child is good at some things and not so good at other things. Just like us, children have ups and downs—good days and bad days. When we appreciate and accept our children, we know the good and the not-so-good. We see the ups and downs. We accept all of these things. We accept our children as they are.

When we do this, our children see that we don't expect them to be perfect. They see that we love and value them.

Some parents think they need to keep pointing out what is wrong. They think this will help children improve. But this can be discouraging.

What if your friend kept telling you, "I know what's wrong with you. I'll tell you, and all you have to do is change!" This is how children feel too.

With encouragement, we accept our children as they are.

Your child will not always do as well as you would like. At those times, children really need your love and acceptance. Children need this no matter how well they do something.

Darnel shows his grandma an outline he made for his social studies paper. Darnel's teacher criticized the outline in some places. Darnel says, "Mr. Firelli didn't like my outline. He said I was missing important information." Grandma looks at the outline. She tells Darnel, "Look at this, Darnel. He says that your ideas for this section are 'on the right track.' And here he says your plan is interesting." "I guess you're right, Gram," says Darnel. "Here he says my plan will work. I guess I just need some more details in some places."

You can accept your child without accepting misbehavior.

Accepting Your Child

- **Think about a bad choice your child has made.**

- **Think of a way to help your child know that he or she is not a bad person.**

- **Think of a way to help your child make a better choice.**

Erika lied to her teacher. She said she left her worksheets at home. The truth was that Erika hadn't done her homework. The teacher called Erika's mother. That night, at bedtime, Mother wanted to talk to Erika about it. Erika cried and said, "I don't know why I'm so bad sometimes." Mother said, "Erika, it was wrong to lie. But you aren't a bad person. You just made a bad choice. Let's talk about what you can do to fix it."

Notice Your Child's Efforts

Improvement takes time. People don't accomplish things all at once.

Think about the first time you gave your baby a bath. Did you feel clumsy? Was it hard to keep the soap out of your child's eyes? Did you wish for a second pair of hands? Yet over time, you found ways to do the job more easily. Maybe you figured out a way to hold your baby with one arm and hand. Maybe you learned to put the soap on the washcloth before you picked the baby up. Maybe you tried sitting down. Maybe you sang gently to your baby. Step by step, you became an expert "baby washer"!

Every skill we learn is made up of small steps and efforts. The same is true as our children learn.

On his first fifth-grade report card, Li has a C in math. His parents know he can do better. They might want to say, "You need to work harder. You should have an A." But how will that help Li?

Li's parents need to encourage Li to improve. To do this, they need to notice his efforts. How?

- They can point out small improvements along the way.

- They can comment positively on a quiz with a B-minus, or homework with a C-plus.

- **They can help Li understand what is important.** *Learning* math is more important than *earning* a letter grade.

Try to find at least one effort or improvement. Look for a chance to tell your child that you have noticed.

Appreciate Your Child

A child needs to contribute—to be a helping part of the family. This gives the child a sense of belonging. When you say and show that you really appreciate your child, you encourage this belonging.

Nellie is 9. Mom feels frustrated when Nellie runs through the living room and hallway. Mom doesn't want to criticize. She wants to find ways to encourage Nellie. So she sits down and thinks about what Nellie has done lately that she appreciates.

Mom thinks of lots of things: Nellie has remembered to take off her snowy boots at the door. She spends time playing with her little brother. Yesterday, Nellie took out the garbage without being asked. All of these things were helpful to Mom.

Mom thinks for only a few minutes. In that short time, she finds many things she appreciates. She decides to start thanking Nellie for cooperating.

Does this mean Mom should let Nellie run in the living room? No. But by stopping to think, Mom helps herself. She stops herself from yelling or punishing. She thinks about her parenting goal. Thinking about what she appreciates helps Mom do this.

Right now, Mom can say to Nellie: "If you want to run, run outside. You decide." Mom also knows that, over time, encouragement will help Nellie cooperate more often. So at other times, Mom can show appreciation when Nellie cooperates. She can say:

- "Thanks for remembering to take off your boots."
- "It's so nice to see you playing with T. J. He really loves his big sister."
- "I appreciated that you took care of the garbage right after school."

There is another way to show appreciation: Notice what is important to your child. Ignoring a child's interest is easy. This is especially true if the interest has never been important to you. But our different interests are part of what makes each of us special. If you take the time to ask about a project, your child will feel appreciated. You might even discover a new interest for yourself!

Your child has *strengths*—qualities and talents that make the child special. You can notice and build on these strengths.

Noticing Improvement

Think about something your child is improving in. Also think of efforts your child has made. For example:

- **Has your child walked away from a fight?**
- **Has your child improved in school?**
- **Has your child found a way to help?**
- **Has your child cooperated with brothers or sisters?**

Juana's stepdad said to Juana, "I like it when you play the guitar. I've never had music around at home before. It's really nice." "I could teach you to play something," Juana said. "Would you? That'd be great!" said her stepdad.

Have Faith in Your Child

Children need to know and see that parents believe they can succeed.

Kara's mom and dad are the caretakers in her apartment building. Every week they mow the lawn. Kara is 11. She wants to run the lawnmower. She asks her dad, "Can I mow the lawn?" Her dad says, "Sure. You can do it with me." Her mom says, "Go put your heavy shoes on." Kara hurries back wearing safe shoes. Her dad says, "First, put on your safety glasses. Then I'll show you how to start the motor."

Kara knows that her parents believe she can learn to mow the lawn. How? Because they tell her that she can. They also take the time to teach her. This will help Kara feel able to try other things as well. It helps her tell herself, "I can do it."

Expectations are powerful. Usually, our children can sense what we really think. Few children will learn to believe in themselves if *we* don't believe in them.

To show faith in your child, you may have to look at the big picture. Don't think about a mistake your child made in the past. Instead, think about the many things your child has learned to do right. Don't worry about a mistake your child might make. Instead, think about the ways you can help your child feel capable.

Growing up is a process. It takes years. Keeping this in mind may help you see that your child *does* learn many skills, over time.

What Is the Difference Between Praise and Encouragement?

Many parents believe they are encouraging children when they really are praising them. Praise can be discouraging.

Praise and encouragement are not the same thing. Each one has a different purpose. As you read about praise and encouragement, remember your parenting goals:

- **to raise a child who is happy, healthy, confident, cooperative, responsible, and loving and lovable**

- to build a strong, lifelong relationship with your child
- to help your child grow to be a responsible adult

Praise Is a Reward

Praise is a type of reward. Children *earn* it. They might earn it by competing and winning. Maybe they earn it by being compared to somebody else. Praise from a parent gives a child the *reward* of being valued by the parent.

It was field day at school. Mark wanted to win a blue ribbon for the fifty-yard dash. Vic, Mark's twin, wanted a blue ribbon for the long jump. Both boys had worked hard to be ready. Mark won a blue ribbon. Vic didn't get a ribbon at all. Mom said to Mark, "You won! Good for you!" Mark was happy. Then he looked at Vic. He said to his mom, "Yeah, but Vic didn't get a ribbon." Mom hugged Mark and said, "Well, he should have worked harder! Everybody can't win." Mark thought, "What if I <u>didn't</u> win? What would Mom think?"

What Does Praise Teach?

With praise, children learn to please others. There is nothing wrong with wanting to please someone. But with a lot of praise, children believe that they *must* please other people. They decide this is the only way to feel worthwhile.

Children also learn to want more and more praise. They may worry when parents do not praise. They start to doubt themselves. They might even think that if they don't get praise, they are getting criticism!

Children may begin to see each activity as a contest to "win" or "lose." They learn that one person can be "better than" someone else. They may even start to believe that competing to win the reward of praise is *everything*.

A child needs encouragement like a plant needs water.

Rudolf Dreikurs

Encouragement Is a Gift

Encouragement is a gift. No one needs to earn it. It is for everyone and can be given for effort or improvement.

A child might be learning to play the trumpet. A parent might say, "That song sounds better than it did a few days ago."

It can be given as a way of noticing what is special.

Later, the parent might say, "It's so nice to hear music every day."

Encouragement can even be given when a child isn't doing well or makes a mistake.

"Yes, you got lost and forgot where you were during your trumpet solo. But you found your place again. It can be hard to think when you're nervous. That's a really important skill you have!"

Encouragement from parents helps children feel valued just for *being*—for being who they are. This helps children accept themselves and feel capable. It raises their self-esteem.

What Does Encouragement Teach?
With encouragement, children learn:

- **to appreciate their own special qualities**
- **to feel capable**
- **to feel worthwhile just the way they are**

Children also learn that they can encourage themselves. They feel more self-confident. Encouraged children are also more interested in cooperating with others.

Praise Uses Words That Judge

"You're such a good kid!" This is not an easy thing to live up to. Hearing this, a child might think, "Am I supposed to be good all the time? What if I'm not good? Am I bad? Am I worthwhile when I'm not doing what Dad wants?"

"You made the team—I'm so proud of you!" A child might hear this as, "You make me look so good! You've pleased me by doing what I want." A child might think, "Am I worthwhile just because I made the team? What if I didn't make the team? Would Mom be disappointed in me?"

Encouragement Uses Words That Notice

Encouragement focuses on how a child has helped. It looks at how the child feels. With encouragement, a parent might say:

- "Thank you for writing such careful phone messages for me!"
- "You seem proud to be on that team!"

To Encourage or to Praise?

- **Children need to learn to cooperate—not to be "better" than others.**

- Children need to feel accepted all the time—not just when they do something right.
- Children need to learn to think for themselves—not to please somebody else.

Using a lot of praise, or only praise, will not help you meet the challenge of parenting.

- We want to teach our children to have faith in themselves.
- We want them to say "I can" and "I will."
- We want them to cooperate and care about others.
- We want them to become self-motivated.

Too much praise can lead to the opposite results.

Encouragement will help you meet your parenting challenge. Most of the time, encouragement is a better choice than praise.

Does this mean that you should never praise your child? No. There are times when praise can be helpful.

Your child just scored. Would you stand up and shout, "You must feel proud of that play"? Of course not. You'd whoop and holler your hurrahs: "Wow! What a shot! Way to go!"

We all like a reward once in a while. When our children work hard and accomplish something, offering our praise is fine. You will be more effective if you avoid praising your child too often. Instead, focus on learning the language of encouragement.

Use the Language of Encouragement

Encouragement has its own language. Here are words that encourage:

- "Thanks. That was a big help."
- "I trust your judgment."
- "That's a tough one, but I think you can work it out."
- "You worked hard on that!"
- "You're getting better at fractions all the time."
- "You can do it."

A Word of Caution

Sometimes parents say something encouraging, but then add something discouraging. For example, a parent might say, "It looks like you really worked hard on that." A child would feel encouraged. But what if the parent added phrases like these?

Thinking About Encouragement

Imagine your child is running a race:

- **What you say at the finish line is praise.**
- **What you say <u>during</u> the race is encouragement.**

Changing to Encouragement

Notice when you praise your child. For example, notice when you say:

- **"You're such a good kid!"**

- **"You did a great job!"**

Think about different words you can use to encourage your child.

- "You worked hard on that . . . I wish you'd do that more often."

- "I trust your judgment . . . so don't let me down."

- "You can do it . . . so quit whining and get busy."

Statements like these give encouragement—and then take it away. The encouragement is lost. Instead, the child feels *dis*couraged. Remember that you are building your child's self-esteem. You are not trying to help your child be perfect!

A Word About Hard Times in a Family

All families have troubles. People get sick or die. Moms and dads lose their jobs. Parents get divorced. When families have trouble,

We all make mistakes. Sometimes this is when we need the most encouragement.

children often struggle too. This is true even for children who usually seem happy and confident. They may not feel good about themselves during these hard times.

This isn't the parents' fault. Parents can't change illness or death. They can't stop job layoffs. A divorce or a new marriage can mean a new start.

A 5 year old's mom remarries a man with two teenagers. Instead of being an only child, the 5 year old is now the youngest of three.

Changes like these may mean that children lose their "place." Then the children have to find a new one. To do this, children may misbehave. This is especially true if the children feel discouraged.

Children may feel guilty. They may think a divorce or a lost job is their fault.

Children may feel angry. They may not want to lose a parent or a sister or brother. They may not want to have a new stepparent or a new stepbrother or stepsister. Some children "act out" by skipping school or doing poorly. They may fight or yell or break things.

Children may feel afraid. They may worry that if one parent leaves, the other will too. They may wonder where money for food will come from.

During these hard family times, children need extra encouragement. They can get encouragement from parents and from other places too. They can get it from your adult friends and relatives. They can get it from a minister. They can get it from groups like Big Brothers or Big Sisters.

If your family is going through a hard time, don't feel guilty. Make an effort to find other adults to help your child. You and your child will both feel better when you do this.

Are There Other Ways to Be Encouraging?

Using helpful words and avoiding too much praise are two important ways to encourage your child. You can do other things too.

Act in Encouraging Ways

We often encourage with words, but our actions can be encouraging too.

A nod, a wink, or a smile sends a message of encouragement. So does listening without interrupting. So does a hug or a pat on the back.

You also show confidence in your child when you allow the child to try something challenging.

Maurice is 11. He wants to ride his bike to the pool with his friends. Dad and Maurice have biked to the pool many times. Dad decides Maurice is ready to go with his friends.

Dad goes over the safety rules with Maurice the night before. Dad says to Maurice, "I know you have biked to the pool before, so you know there is traffic. I'd like to go over some safety rules." Dad talks and then listens. Maurice feels respected. Dad feels sure

Maurice is ready to be responsible. The next day as Maurice leaves with his friends, Dad smiles and says, "Have a good time."

You also show confidence when you let your child tackle a problem alone. Be sure it is possible for your child to do the problem. It will depend on the problem and your child's age. If children need help, parents can still let them be "in charge."

Lisa and her friend Julie have been having trouble getting along. Lisa says to her dad, "I don't know why Julie's being so mean. I wish she'd stop it." Dad sees that Lisa feels hurt. "You feel hurt when Julie treats you badly." Lisa nods. Dad says, "Have you thought about talking to her?"

"I don't know what to say," says Lisa. Dad says, "Why don't you think about that for a while, Lisa? You can try some things out on me, if you want to."

Dad knows he can't solve Lisa's problem. Lisa needs to learn to talk through problems with friends. But Dad has shown Lisa that he believes she can do this. He has encouraged her to think of ideas on her own. He has let her know he'll be glad to help.

In Chapter 5, you will learn more about solving problems with your child.

Teach Respect for Others

Self-esteem is extremely important. So is "people esteem"—feeling and showing respect for others. Truly respecting ourselves is hard if we don't respect others.

This means that teaching and showing respect is a way to encourage your child. There are many ways to do this.

Help Other People
Make an effort to help friends and neighbors. The job might be large, such as helping someone move. It might be small.

You and your child might water plants when a neighbor is gone. You might fix a meal for the family of a friend who is sick.

Look for opportunities to volunteer as a family too.

Your child's school might have a food drive. You could help your child collect canned goods.

Teach Manners
Being polite is not old-fashioned. We all appreciate being treated politely. Model the behaviors you want in your child. Say "please" and "thank you" to your children:

- "Please clear your dishes before you leave."
- "Thanks for putting away the laundry."

Expect your children to treat you politely too. Begin by telling them what you expect. If they forget, don't nag. Instead, offer gentle reminders.

Courtney says to her stepdad, "Can I have a glass of juice?" He gives Courtney the juice and says, "You're welcome." Courtney smiles and says, "Oh, yeah—thank you." Dad says, "I expect please and thank you. If you forget next time, I just won't respond to the request."

Appreciate That People Are Different
Our world is full of people who are different from one another. We come from large families and small families. We are of different races, religions, and values. We enjoy different activities. We have different interests, talents, and abilities.

Teach your child to appreciate these differences, and show that you appreciate them.

See the Good Side

You've seen how goals for attention, power, revenge, and display of inadequacy have a "flip side." This is true for other things too. Look for the positive in what seems to be a problem. Look at a stubborn child as determined, or a child who is easily hurt as sensitive. Recognizing this alternative ("flip side") is a good way to work on not criticizing.

Encourage Yourself

Things take time. To help your child grow in self-esteem might take time. During this time, you need to keep encouraging your child. You may find it hard to do this if your child is not responding as you wish. If this happens, it's time to encourage yourself. You are learning new parenting skills. You are making changes in how you speak and act. As you do, give yourself the gift of encouragement.

Have Patience With Yourself
We often think of learning as a one-way trip. This trip goes *up*, like a car climbing up a hill. But learning doesn't really happen like this. Instead, it is more like the ocean tide. When the tide comes in, it comes forward. Then it falls back and comes forward again.

The falling back can feel discouraging. It helps to remember this: Each time you move forward, you are ahead of where you were the last time.

Remember That Your Child Is Not You

Your child is not a sign of your own success or failure.

- Sometimes things will go well for your child. Then you can feel happy for your child rather than proud for yourself.
- Sometimes things won't go well for your child. Then you can show that you understand. You don't need to feel like a failure as a parent.

Set Realistic Goals

Don't set goals for yourself—or your child—that are sure to discourage you. It is good for each of us to remind ourselves of all the ways we are growing as parents.

Jack, who is 10, says to his mom, "I hate being fat." Mom knows Jack needs to lose weight and get more exercise. She says to Jack, "I'll be glad to help you lose weight. We could all eat better around here." Mom doesn't take every sweet or fatty food out of the kitchen. She doesn't sign Jack up for aerobics five days a week. Mom knows that pushing Jack won't help him feel good about himself. She knows it won't help her either.

Instead, Mom starts to change the family's meals and snacks a little at a time. She buys more fruit and fewer cookies. She looks for ways to encourage Jack to get some exercise: She asks him to take the dog all the way to the park for a good run. She asks him to go downstairs for the mail. She suggests a walk together on the weekend. In these ways, she helps Jack feel good about himself. She helps him to help himself.

Use Positive Self-Talk

In Chapter 2 you looked at your self-talk and your beliefs and feelings. Use self-talk to give yourself encouragement in small doses. Do this as often as you can. Encourage yourself both as a parent and as a person:

- "I handled Ronnie and Susie's fight calmly."
- "I didn't yell today."
- "I listened to what Josef was saying."

Be as Healthy as You Can

Working to stay healthy will help you handle your own feelings and your child's behavior better. It also shows your child that taking care of one's health is important.

Accepting and Valuing Yourself

Take some time to think about all the things you like about yourself:

- **What is unique about you?**
- **When do you feel most capable?**
- **When are you happiest?**
- **What qualities are you glad you have?**

Keep a list in your purse or pocket. Add to it whenever you can. Let your list keep growing.

When you feel discouraged, read your list!

Use self-talk to give yourself the encouragement you need.

Do your best to eat balanced meals and get some kind of exercise every day. This might be a daily walk or ten minutes of exercise on the living room floor. Encourage your child to join you.

Look for healthy things to do as a family. Go hiking or biking. Play volleyball. Walk when doing errands.

Use your time valuably. You can't say yes to every request for your time. Part of staying healthy is learning to say no. This shows your children that they can learn to control their time too.

Have the Courage to Be Imperfect

You know that you can't expect your child to grow in self-esteem all at once. You can't expect yourself to grow as a parent all at once either. You and your children are human beings. You are not perfect. In fact, you never will be!

Earlier, we talked about the word *courage.* Rudolf Dreikurs had an idea he called "the courage to be imperfect." With the courage to be imperfect, you are willing to make an effort. You quit worrying about what happened in the past. You focus on what is happening today.

- Work at being helpful—not better than others.

- See mistakes as part of learning.

- Enjoy yourself and other people. This feels much better than finding fault.

Encouragement
STEP

This week, make a special effort to show <u>acceptance</u> of your child. Notice how this can help build your child's self-confidence.

Be aware of times you want to judge or criticize. Find a way to show support instead. For example, you might say:

- "I know you have trouble getting along with the coach. What do you think you can do to make practice go more smoothly?"

- "I know you don't like doing the dishes. That was a good idea you had to listen to the radio while you work."

- "I know being patient at the doctor's office was hard for you. Thanks for making the effort."

Plan <u>when</u> you will do this and <u>what</u> you will say or do.

For Your *Family*

Brainstorm ideas for having fun together. To brainstorm, have everyone suggest ideas. Stay open-minded. Sometimes ideas sound silly or impossible. Don't be quick to judge them. One "silly" idea might help someone think of another really good one.

Choose at least one way to have fun together as a family. Plan what you will do and when you will do it. Then follow through. Have fun!

- Make small changes—not try to be a whole new you.
- Get to know your own strengths and good qualities.
- Value yourself.
- See parenting as a challenge to be met—not a problem to overcome.

You Have Taken Another Big Step

In Chapter 3, you have learned many ways to help your child and yourself:

- You have seen how self-esteem and encouragement are connected.
- You have found ways to show acceptance, faith, and appreciation.
- You have learned the difference between praise and encouragement.
- You have seen that too much praise can be discouraging.
- You have learned and practiced the language of encouragement.
- You have considered many ways to show encouragement.
- You have found the courage to be imperfect.

This week, find ways to encourage your child. Find as many ways as you can. Each time, notice:

- what happened
- how you encouraged your child
- how your child responded

JUST FOR YOU

Self-Encouragement

Encouraging yourself is just as important as encouraging your children. If you don't feel encouraged, encouraging your children is harder too. It's a matter of "I can't give what I don't have."

When you feel encouraged, you lose your fear of failure. You see your abilities more clearly. One way to encourage yourself is to think, write, and believe ideas such as:

- I am a positive person.
- I am a capable person.
- I am capable of change.
- I love myself.

Think about these encouraging ideas. What do they mean to you? What else can you say to yourself? Think of one more encouraging idea that applies to you.

Remind yourself of these beliefs. Write them down and post them on a mirror or keep them in your wallet or purse.

POINTS TO REMEMBER

1. Encouragement is a skill to help children grow in self-esteem. It shows that they are important, capable, and loved.

2. You encourage when you:
   - love and accept your child
   - notice your child's efforts
   - appreciate your child
   - have faith in your child

3. Praise is a reward that children earn. It teaches them to please others.

4. Encouragement is a gift. Everyone deserves it. It can be given for effort. It can be given when a child is not doing well. And it can be given just for *being*.

5. Encourage your child as often as you can.

6. Children need extra encouragement during hard family times.

7. You also encourage children when you show respect for yourself and for others.

8. Setting realistic goals will encourage both you and your child.

Chart 3
THE LANGUAGE OF ENCOURAGEMENT

Words that say "I accept you"	Words that say "I know you can"	Words that say "I see that you are working and improving"	Words that say "I appreciate you"
"You seem to like chess a lot."	"You can do it. You've made it partway already."	"You worked hard on that!"	"I needed your help and you came through."
"How do you feel about it?"	"You're making progress."	"You're getting better at fractions all the time."	"Thanks. That was a big help."
"I can tell you're pleased about it."	"I trust your judgment."	"Look at the progress you've made."	"It was thoughtful of you to do that."
"I can see you're not satisfied. What do you think you can do so you'll feel happier with it?"	"That's a tough one, but I think you can work it out."	"Looks like you spent a lot of time thinking that through."	"I really appreciate when you help me. It makes grocery shopping a lot easier."
"It looks like you enjoyed that."	"I need your help fixing this."	"I see you're moving along."	"I need your help planning the picnic."
"You did your best—that's all anyone can do."	"You'll figure it out."	"You may not feel you've reached your goal, but look how far you've come."	"You have skill in _____. Would you do that for the family?"
"I enjoy your sense of humor."	"Knowing you, I'm sure you'll do fine."		"I really enjoyed our game. Thanks."
"It's nice that you enjoy learning."			

Developing the Courage to Be Imperfect

You are almost halfway done with STEP. Sometimes, parents feel guilty at this point. You might feel as if you have been raising your children "wrong." Be patient with yourself. Remember your parenting goals:

- **to raise a child who is happy, confident, cooperative, and responsible**
- **to form a strong bond among family members**
- **to raise a child who is loved and able to give love**

We can add one more important idea that helps you with these goals. It is the courage to be imperfect.* With this courage, you can:

1. Encourage your children to make efforts, not to expect perfection.

2. Look at mistakes as ways to learn, not failures.

3. Understand mistakes as a part of being human—you'll always make them.

4. Do what you can, and accept your efforts.

5. Take the next good step.

6. Develop your own personal strengths and worth.

7. Develop mutual respect by valuing yourself.

8. Develop the courage to cope with life's challenges.

By reading this book, you send a clear signal that you are willing to consider new ideas. It is a sign of growth. Know this, and encourage yourself as you continue to progress!

---

*Dr. Rudolf Dreikurs, an internationally known psychiatrist, originally developed the idea of the courage to be imperfect.

Listening
and **Talking**
to Your Child

Communication is the key to most relationships. Think about what this means in a friendship. Friends talk together. They listen to each other. By listening and sharing, the friendship grows.

When our friends have problems or make mistakes, we consider their feelings. We listen and try to help. We do this because we respect and value our friends.

We want to treat our children the same way. It builds a closer relationship.

When you are upset, you might talk to a friend. You want your friend to listen, understand, and accept what you are feeling. When upset, this is what your child wants too.

Sometimes a parent wants to "fix" the problem. It's natural to feel this way. Does it help?

A parent might say, "You shouldn't be angry." Or, "Shame on you for yelling like that." Or, "Don't be such a baby." When we say this, a child might hear, "My feelings are bad." "My mom thinks I'm bad."

A parent might say, "Don't worry. It will turn out all right." A child might hear, "My dad doesn't understand how important this is."

We can't always "fix" a problem. We also can't make our child's feelings go away. What can we do? We can show that we care. We can show that we understand and accept the child's feelings, even if we disagree with the child. We show acceptance by our tone of voice and by the words we use. We communicate respect. This is better than giving advice, which doesn't help children solve problems. With advice, the child may rely on us or ignore the advice. When we listen, we give the child room to think.

Here's what you will learn . . .

- **To have a good relationship, talk together using special skills.**
- **You can listen to hear how your child is feeling.**
- **You can show your child that talking about feelings is okay.**
- **You can talk about problems without blaming.**

How Can I Be a Good Listener?

Communication has two parts: listening and talking. To help your child communicate with you, listen carefully and speak respectfully to your child.

Treat your child just like you'd treat your best friend.

Listen for Feelings

Why is listening for feelings important? It helps children know they are understood. It helps them think about what they are feeling and why. It can help them think through a problem. It lets children know that talking about feelings is okay.

How to Listen for Feelings

Listening for feelings is a special skill. It is called *reflective listening.* Here is how you do it:

1.   Listen. Let your body show that you are listening. You might have to bend down. You might sit next to your child. Stop your other tasks. Look at your child. Pay full attention to your child.

2.   Hear the feeling. Listen to your child's words. Ask yourself, "What is my child feeling?" Think of a word that describes the feeling. Also ask yourself, "Why is my child feeling this way? What led to the feeling?"

3.   Use reflective listening. Reflective listening is repeating what you think your child feels and says. Think of yourself as a mirror that *reflects* your child's feelings. You also reflect the *reason* behind the feeling.

To listen reflectively, start by using the words "You feel" before the feeling, and "because" to tell the reason for the feeling:

- "*You feel* jealous *because* Mike got picked and you didn't."
- "*You feel* disappointed *because* Petra didn't call."
- "*You feel* impatient *because* you want to use the phone."

After a while, reflective listening will feel more natural. Then you can use your own words:

- "Are you hurt that Carlo didn't ask you to the party?"
- "You're lonesome in our new apartment."
- "Looks like you're eager to get to practice."

Describe the feeling as exactly as you can. Words like "a little" or "very" will help you here:

- "You seem a little worried about how you did on the test."

- "You're very angry that I said you had to stay home."
- "It seems like no one cares, and you're feeling very left out."

Sarah and her stepdaughter Carrie went to a carnival. They rode rides and ate treats. When it was time to leave, Carrie begged and whined. "We can't go yet," she cried. "I haven't ridden the rocket!" Sarah said to her, "You're unhappy because we have to go. It's hard to leave when you're having fun."

Sarah could have said to Carrie, "Stop whining. Why do you have to spoil our day like this?" But then Carrie might not remember the fun she and Sarah had. She might just remember that Sarah had "spoiled" things. Instead, Sarah let Carrie know she understood how she felt. She gave Carrie a chance to end their day remembering what a good time it was.

Look for Feelings Too

Children don't always use words to communicate. Sometimes they are silent, but they smile, or scowl, or cry. Sometimes they pull away or hang their head. As with listening to words, ask yourself, "What is my child feeling?" Look at what your child's face and body are telling you. Then state the feeling you see:

- "Your frown seems to say that you disagree."
- "When your face lights up like that, you look very happy."
- "It looks like you're really upset. Want to talk about it?"

Children don't always use words to tell us how they feel.

Words for "Happy" Feelings	Words for "Upset" Feelings
appreciated	angry
better	bored
comfortable	confused
excited	disappointed
grateful	frustrated
great	guilty
happy	hurt
pleased	left out
proud	put down
relieved	miserable
satisfied	worthless

Finding the Feelings

Three feeling words parents can overuse are "good," "bad," and "upset." These words don't always tell the whole story.

Look at the word lists above. Use these words when they describe your child's feelings.

Some Things to Keep in Mind

Listening for feelings may be new to both you and your child. Here are some hints as you begin.

Your child may be surprised. Your child will probably notice your new way of listening. A child might say, "Yeah, that's right," and then walk away. Don't force your child to share feelings. Your child might think you are snooping. Pushing the child to talk could lead to a power struggle.

Don't be discouraged if the child doesn't respond quickly. Instead, wait for another chance to listen and talk about feelings. Your child may want to talk. If so, you might ask, "Would you like to tell me more about it?"

Use a respectful questioning tone. You can't be sure you know exactly what your child is feeling:

Shonda came in from school and slammed the door. She went straight to the couch and sat down. She scowled. Her dad said to her, "Bad day at school, huh?"

"School was okay," said Shonda. "But I <u>hate</u> riding that <u>stupid</u> bus!" Dad sat down next to Shonda. He said, "You sound very angry. Do you want to tell me about it?"

Dad thought Shonda had a problem at school. His guess was wrong. Because of his tone of voice, Shonda could tell he cared and wanted to help. So she told him a little more. He didn't tell her not to yell. He let Shonda know she could talk with him some more.

Check your own feelings. At times, listening for feelings can go too far. It might even become part of a child's goal of misbehavior. If you think this might be happening, check your own feeling. Are you annoyed? angry? discouraged?

Jerod was working on a social studies paper. All weekend he kept coming to his mom complaining about it. Each time, Mom listened and tried to understand how Jerod was feeling. By Sunday afternoon, she felt annoyed and thought that Jerod wanted her attention—not her help. So she said to him, "We've talked about this a lot this weekend. I guess I can't help you with it. But I know you'll be able to finish your paper." Then Mom took the Sunday paper into the kitchen. She didn't say anything more.

Mom saw that Jerod wanted too much attention. She decided not to give it, but stayed respectful. Jerod was probably not pleased. But he could see that Mom respected him. Mom let Jerod know that he must be willing to work on his own problem. She has shown confidence in him.

Reflective listening helps when you have to say no. Sometimes you have to say no to your child. When you do, your child may become upset. Listen to what your child is feeling. Give feedback. Then your child will know you have heard the feelings:

- "I can see that you're angry, but throwing things is not okay. I'll be in the kitchen if you'd like to talk about it."
- "You're disappointed. You don't think I'm being fair. But I can't send you on the camp-out with a fever."

If your child tries to argue, leave the room. When your child's mood is better, do something fun together.

When we respond in this way, children may not be any happier. But they learn that their feelings are still okay—even when their actions aren't.

Reflective listening isn't always necessary. Your child's response won't always be about feelings:

- "Yeah—pizza!" This doesn't need any feedback.
- "Can I wait to do my chores until after lunch?" This might just be a direct request.

Sometimes you won't be able to talk when your child wants to. Tell the child you can talk later: "You're worried and want to talk about this. Right now, I have to finish my work. Let's talk about it during supper."

Give It Some Time

Reflective listening may not feel natural at first. Remember *why* you are doing it: To show your child that you hear, understand, and accept the feelings. Taking time to think before you talk can help you too. You won't say something you don't really want to say.

Like any new skill, reflective listening will take time and practice. Keep at it! After a while, it will begin to feel more natural. You will see how it helps you and your child. You may find that you understand each other better.

How Can I Talk So My Child Will Listen?

You have seen how reflective listening and talking go together: You listen for feelings. Then you give feedback. Let's look at how to tell your child about *your* feelings.

Speak With Respect

When you have a problem with your child, you need to talk about it. When you do, share your feelings respectfully.

Diego and Ramón are brothers. They are wrestling in the living room while Mom and her friend are talking seriously. Mom is beginning to feel angry. She wants to yell, "You two are acting like monsters! Cut it out!"

What if we treated our friends the way we sometimes treat our children?

But Mom thinks before she speaks. She says to her friend, "Excuse me a minute." She says to her boys, "When you wrestle and make noise, I feel discouraged because Ray and I can't hear each other. You may find something quiet to do in here. Or you may take the roughhousing to your room. You decide."

Mom felt like yelling. But she knew that would only show Diego and Ramón that yelling is a way to solve problems. The boys were already "wound up." If Mom yelled, it might have grown into a power struggle.

Instead, Mom chose to be respectful. She didn't judge the boys by calling them names. She understood they wanted to play. Her response told them that her need for quiet was important.

Will Ramón and Diego behave? If they do, Mom might later tell them, "I appreciated how you quieted down when Ray and I were talking." If they don't, Mom needs to keep using respectful words: "I see you've decided to go to your room. I'll walk there with you." Then Mom could simply walk with the boys to their room. She doesn't need to say another thing.

Hearing respectful words will encourage Diego and Ramón. It will teach them a way to speak to other people when they disagree with others' behavior.

What kind of respectful words can we use? One way to talk about problems is with an "I-message."

You-Messages Put Children Down

When talking to children, we can use "you-messages" and "I-messages." You-messages put down, blame, or nag. Often they use the word *you:*

- "You should know better."
- "You stop that."
- "You cut it out!"

What Do Children Learn?

Children who hear too many you-messages begin to feel discouraged. They may fight back, feel worthless, stop listening. You-messages can lower self-esteem, don't teach children to cooperate, and are discouraging.

I-Messages Show Respect

A better way to talk about a problem is with an I-message. I-messages tell how you feel when a child ignores your rights. They focus on you, rather than the child. I-messages don't label or blame. When you use an I-message, you simply tell how you feel.

I-Messages Have Three Parts

To use an I-message, do three things:

1. Tell what is *happening*.

2. Tell what you *feel*.

3. *Explain* why you feel that way.

Here is an I-message:

- "When you don't call, I feel worried because I don't know where you are."

It uses these words:

1.	When	"*When* you don't call,
2.	I feel	*I feel* worried
3.	because	*because* I don't know where you are."

Once you understand the parts of an I-message, use words that feel natural to you:

- "I feel scared when I find the iron left on. We could have a fire."

Decide if you want to tell about your feeling, or just the problem:

- "I can't set the table when it's covered with toys."

These are the most important things to remember about I-messages:

- They focus on *you*, not your child.

- They do not place blame on anyone.

What Do Children Learn?

I-messages help children hear what their actions mean to you. Children hear a way to talk about problems without blaming. They learn to share feelings in a way that can help solve a problem.

An I-message also shows respect for you. It lets you be honest about how you feel and what you want. It shows respect for your child. It also shows that you expect cooperation.

Look for the Real Problem

At first, it might seem hard to explain your feelings with an I-message. Thinking about this might help: Most of the time, what bothers us is not what children *do*. What bothers us is the *result* of what they do.

Janet often doesn't brush her teeth. Her parents worry about cavities and bleeding gums. They worry about dental bills. They worry that Janet's friends will make fun of her bad breath.

Yes, it is important for Janet to brush her teeth. But what really bothers Janet's parents? Is it what can happen because of not brushing?

A focus on the results and how they feel about them helps Janet's parents. They will find better words to talk about the problem. They don't say, "You must brush your teeth, or else!" Instead, they might say:

"When you don't brush, we worry about what will happen to your teeth. It's no fun to have cavities filled."

Give Choices

We can give choices with our words. Remember Ramón and Diego roughhousing in the living room? Mom can add a choice to her I-message, saying, "You can play quietly in here or take your loud play to your room or outside. You decide." These words give her sons choices about what and where they can play. She also showed that she expected her sons to cooperate.

Be Careful When You Are Angry

Keeping angry feelings out of your I-messages is important. Anger makes it hard for children *not* to feel blamed for the anger.

We don't mean that you should never be angry with your child. But expressing anger too often creates problems:

A child might seek more power or revenge. When you get angry, the child knows the attempts to be the boss or get even are working.

A child might feel threatened and quit talking to you. Good relationships need communication.

To move away from anger:
- Give an I-message *before* you feel really angry. For example, you might start out feeling worried, scared, or disappointed. You could talk to your child at that point, using an I-message. This way you may avoid getting more upset.
- Focus on your beliefs and on changing your angry feelings. Chapter 2 gives many ideas to help you do this.
- Look for times to talk with your child when you are not angry. Find times to have fun together.

The Three Parts of an I-Message

I-messages use these words:

1. **When**　"**When** the floor is wet,
2. **I feel**　**I feel** worried
3. **because**　**because** someone might slip and get hurt."

For Your *Family*

Spend a few minutes talking about a problem. For now, choose one that isn't too big. Help your family find a new way to look at the problem. Start by showing them a way to do this. Here's an example:

Angie might say, "Ben's selfish! He won't share!" You might say, "Ben likes chips a lot. Maybe he just eats them up without thinking. Ben, did you know that Angie wants chips too?"

Ben may know very well that Angie wants chips. It's okay to give him an "out" here. This lets everyone take a fresh look at the problem. It helps Ben think about sharing without being put down. It shows Angie a way to talk to Ben that might work better for her.

I'm Really Angry—What Should I Do?

1. **Get away from your child.** Leave the room. Go for a walk. Call a friend. If you can't leave your child alone, call a friend and ask for help.

2. **Seek help for yourself.** If you are so angry that you are afraid you will hurt your child, people in the helping professions can help you.

Be Ready to Listen

When you give an I-message about a problem, your child might want to talk about it. Then you will want to use all your communication skills.

Mary's best friend Tia moved away. A few weeks later, Mary's dad got a big phone bill. He said to Mary, "I was shocked to see this phone bill. Our budget isn't big enough for so many long-distance calls." Mary said, "But, Dad, Tia's lonesome. She doesn't know anybody in her new town. I promised her I'd call a lot."

Dad said, "Sounds like you really miss her too. It's pretty hard to have your best friend move away." "Yeah," said Mary, "and I try to talk for a short time, but it always goes so fast."

"Have you thought about other ways to stay in touch?" Dad asked. Then Dad and Mary talked some more. They decided Mary could talk to Tia for ten minutes twice a month. For the rest of the time, Mary and Tia could tape-record messages and send them in the mail.

Here, Dad's I-message opened the door for Mary and her dad to talk. Lots of good things happened. Dad saw that Mary was missing her friend. Mary saw that Dad cared about her problems. Dad also showed Mary that they could talk through problems.

Sometimes, Simply Ask

You can't use I-messages all of the time. If you use them every time your child does something you don't like, your child may quit listening. Sometimes a simple request is the best way to gain cooperation:

*   "Would you please feed the cat?"
*   "It would help if you clean the tub after your bath."
*   "Please lock the door as soon as you come inside."

Send Friendly I-Messages Too

Children love to hear friendly I-messages! They are a wonderful way to encourage:

- "It sure feels good to come home to your cheerful smile today."
- "I noticed that you put away the laundry. Thank you."

Listening for feelings and using I-messages will help you communicate with your child. These skills will help you guide, not control, your child. With many children, building respect and trust takes a long time. Don't give up. Keep in mind your parenting challenge:

- to raise a child who is happy, healthy, confident, cooperative, and responsible
- to build a strong, lifelong relationship with your child
- to help your child grow to be a responsible adult
- to raise a child who is loved and able to give love

Encouragement
STEP

Notice when your child does things that are helpful. Notice when he or she is responsible. Give friendly I-messages, or say "I noticed." Here are some examples:

- **"I noticed that you vacuumed after eating popcorn in the living room."**
- **"I noticed that you were patient with your little sister."**

Sometimes it's hard to keep anger out of your I-messages.

You Have Taken Another Big Step

In Chapter 4, you have learned communication skills and how they can help you build a better relationship with your child.

- You have found that listening for feelings shows your child that you understand. It also helps your child talk about feelings and work through problems.

- You have seen that you can look as well as listen for feelings.

- You have learned a way to tell how you feel without blaming or judging.

- You have added ways to respect your child and to be respected.

THIS WEEK

Start to notice what you *first* want to say when your child talks to you or misbehaves. Stop yourself from talking without thinking.

Instead, think of respectful ways to talk with your child. Do these as often as you can:

- Use reflective listening.
- Use I-messages.

JUST FOR YOU

Conflict in Adult Relationships

Conflict with other adults can be extremely stressful. Talking it through by exploring alternatives can help when you have a conflict with your spouse, a relative, coworkers, or a friend.

Using the five steps you will learn in Chapter 5 is helpful in your adult relationships. Also be willing to consider these ideas:

- Keep mutual respect for each other.

- Believe the problem can be resolved. Be willing to give 100 percent to resolving it.

- Identify the real issue. The words of the conflict may be about money or chores. The *real* issue is often who's right, who's the boss, or fairness.

- In a conflict, the people involved have "agreed to fight." Change the agreement by changing your behavior.

- Be willing to compromise. Invite participation in decision making.

POINTS TO REMEMBER

1. Communication is important for your relationship with your child.

2. Children want parents to hear, understand, and accept their feelings.

3. When you use reflective listening, you reflect your child's feeling and the reason for the feeling. Start by using the words "You feel" and "because":
   - "*You feel* jealous *because* Mike got picked and you didn't."
   - "*You feel* disappointed *because* Petra didn't call."

4. You-messages put down or blame children.

5. I-messages tell how you feel without blaming. To use an I-message, tell what is happening, what you feel, and why you feel that way. It uses these words:
   - When   "*When* you don't call,
   - I feel   *I feel* worried
   - because   *because* I don't know where you are."

6. Avoid using angry I-messages.

7. If you are really angry, get away from your child. Calm down or get some help.

8. Building respect and trust takes a long time. Don't give up.

Chart 4
YOU-MESSAGES AND I-MESSAGES

You-Message	I-Message
"Why can't you clean up the kitchen like you're supposed to? I'm not your maid!"	"When the kitchen's not cleaned up, I feel let down. It seems like people expect me to do all the work."
"Just once could you get to the bus stop on time?"	"I need for you to be on time for the bus. When I have to worry about how to get you to school, I'm late for work."
"Who told you to wear your good clothes to play outside?"	"When you play in your good clothes, they wear out quickly. I get concerned because we can't afford to buy more clothes."
"Don't you talk to me like that!"	"I don't feel respected when I hear words like those."
"Can't you see I'm busy?"	"I'm in the middle of something right now. I'd appreciate if you would wait a minute."

CHAPTER FIVE

Helping
Children
Cooperate

We want our children to grow to be responsible adults. To live, work, and play with others, they must learn to cooperate. One of our jobs as parents is to teach cooperation. An important way we do this is by cooperating ourselves. This shows our children what cooperation means.

What Is Cooperation?

Cooperation means working together. It doesn't mean that children do what adults order them to do. This chapter looks at many ways to teach our children cooperation. It will show you how your family can cooperate to solve problems. You will also see that cooperating can make family life more fun.

How Can I Help My Child Cooperate?

When you have a problem with your child, decide how to deal with it. First, ask yourself, "Who does this problem belong to? Me? Or my child?" In other words, who "owns" the problem?

Decide Who Owns the Problem

To decide who owns a problem, ask yourself four questions:
1. Are my rights being disrespected?
2. Could anybody get hurt?

Here's what you will learn . . .

- **Cooperating means working together.**

- **Children can be responsible for some of their own problems.**

- **You and your child can talk together and solve problems.**

- **Family meetings help families enjoy each other and solve problems together.**

3. Are someone's belongings threatened?

4. Is my child too young to be responsible for this problem?

- If the answer to *any* of these questions is yes, then you own the problem.

- If the answer to *every* question is no, then your child owns the problem.

Sofie is 11. Her brother Misha is 9. They are outside playing with friends. Dad looks out and sees his two kids arguing about who is "It." Dad watches for a minute. Then he leaves the window. Dad knows that Misha and Sofie own this problem.

- What if the children had been arguing inside? If the noise bothered Dad, his rights would not be respected. Then he would own the problem.

- What if the children had started kicking and hitting? If someone could be hurt, then Dad would own the problem.

- What if Misha was only 3 years old? A three year old can sometimes own a problem. But not when the other person is so much older and stronger. Dad would own the problem if one of the children was so young. After separating the kids, Dad could say, "If you can't play without hitting, you'll need to be apart. Let me know when you can solve your problem without hitting."

The person who owns a problem is responsible for solving it. Does this mean you shouldn't help your child solve a problem? No. Sometimes you will want to help your child. But if the problem belongs to a child, then the child is in charge of it.

Ten-year-old Julio is on the phone with a friend. His grandmother can hear that they are arguing. She hears Julio cry, "That's not fair! No way!" He sounds mad. Grandmother doesn't say, "What's going on? What's wrong?" She doesn't try to talk to Julio's friend. She knows that Julio owns the problem of getting along with his friend.

Sometimes the Parent Owns the Problem

Let's look at some problems owned by the parent:

Rudeness to Mom

Heather is 7. She has started to be rude to her mom. In the car on the way to the library, Heather told her friend, "My mom is the stupidest lady in the world." Mom feels hurt by this. She feels mad too. Mom has a right to be treated with respect. So Mom owns this problem.

What Can Mom Do?

- Mom can think about Heather's goal. Mom may think Heather wants to get even. If so, she can do something Heather doesn't expect. She might just ignore the rudeness for a while.

- Later, when they are alone, Mom can use an I-message to tell Heather how she feels: "When you call me names, I feel discouraged. It seems like you don't respect me."

- Mom can use reflective listening with Heather: "It sounds like you're really mad at me. Can we talk about it?" If Heather is willing, she and Mom can talk the problem through.

- Mom can give Heather a choice: "I will drive you to the library if you can be respectful. Otherwise, you can stay home. You decide."

Trouble on the Bus

Owen is 11. He rides the bus to school. Mom got a phone call from the bus driver. He told her that Owen has been making trouble on the bus. He and some other kids have been shouting and fighting. Owen has thrown books and pushed people. The bus driver has told Owen he will be reported if he fights on the bus again.

Mom doesn't want her son to fight and make trouble. She doesn't know what she'll do if he gets kicked off the bus. School is across town. She will have to leave earlier to get Owen to school and still get to work on time.

Someone could get hurt if there's fighting. Mom owns this problem. But that doesn't let Owen off the hook.

What Can Mom Do?

- Mom can talk with Owen. She can tell him about the bus driver's call. She can ask what is happening. Owen might be looking for power. Or, he might be fighting because he is afraid of the other boys. Talking will help Mom find out what is going on.

- Mom can tell Owen his choices: to follow the bus rules or be kicked off the bus.

Mom can't make Owen follow the rules. She can't change the consequence of being kicked off the bus. If that happens, Owen must still go to school. They would have to leave earlier, so she could get to work. Then Owen would have a consequence of getting up extra early.

Being a parent is not easy. When children misbehave, life can get complicated. Hard as it may be, this mom will need to keep her goal in mind:

- to raise a child who is happy, healthy, confident, cooperative, and loved and loving
- to build a strong, lifelong relationship with her child
- to help her child grow to be a responsible adult

Sometimes the Child Owns the Problem

Now let's look at some problems that the child owns.

Nobody Likes Me

Bill's dad came in the door from work. Bill was sitting in front of the TV, crying. "You must be watching something pretty sad," his dad said to him. "It's not the TV," cried Bill. "It's Thai and Artie. They went to play ball. They didn't even call me. Nobody likes me." Bill began to cry harder.

Dad felt bad. But he knew he couldn't fix this problem. Dad knew that Bill owned the problem of getting along with friends.

What Can Dad Do?

- Dad can keep listening to Bill's feelings.
- If Bill wants help, Dad can help him think of ways to get along with friends. He can let Bill know that he loves and respects him. But Dad can't change how Bill's friends act. Making and keeping friends is something Bill has to do for himself.

A School Project

Brian and his brother share a bedroom. It is always a real mess. Brian has been collecting leaves for a school project. He has to put the leaves in a book and write about them. When he is ready to put the book together, he can't find all of his leaves. The few leaves that he has found are torn and crumpled. He runs to his mom and says, "I can't find my leaves! You've gotta help me!"

Brian's schoolwork is his job. So is taking care of his part of the bedroom. This problem belongs to Brian.

What Can Mom Do?

- Right now, Mom really cannot—or should not—do anything to save Brian's project. The consequence of a bad grade may be an important lesson for him. If Mom helps him dig through his messy room, what will Brian learn? He'll learn that he doesn't need to be responsible. He'll learn that Mom can "save" him from his own bad choices.

Thinking About Who Owns the Problem

Think about a problem that is happening with your child. Ask yourself:

1. Are my rights being disrespected?

2. Could anybody get hurt?

3. Are someone's belongings threatened?

4. Is my child too young to be responsible for the problem?

- If the answer to <u>any</u> of these questions is yes, then you own the problem.

- If the answer to <u>every</u> question is no, then your child owns the problem.

Decide who owns the problem—you or your child.

Thinking these things through is one way you show respect to your child and yourself.

Many problems can be solved if you and your child cooperate. This is true no matter who owns the problem.

● At another time, though, Mom can talk to Brian about taking care of his things. She might say, "For school projects, it helps to be organized. Would you like to talk about some ideas to do that?" If Brian wants to talk, he and his mom might have a lot of ideas to share.

Let children own the problem of getting along with each other. Their solutions might surprise you!

How Can My Child and I Solve Problems Together?

Deciding who owns problems helps you know what to do. It helps your child become independent. If you own the problem, you need to take action. If your child owns the problem, you might want to let your child cope alone. Or, you might want to help your child solve it.

You've already learned many things to do when there's a problem. You might:

● Ignore the problem.

● Use reflective listening.

● Use an I-message.

● Help your child see the choices and the possible consequences.

Asking Open Questions

Think of a problem you are having with your child. To understand how your child views the problem, use open questions. Use these words to start open questions:

- **Where?**
- **When?**
- **What?**
- **Who?**
- **Which?**
- **How?**

Practice asking open questions. Work to keep your tone of voice, body, and face respectful. You want to show respect for yourself and your child.

Another way to solve a problem is to talk it through with your child. You take the time to listen, talk, and agree about a way to solve the problem. This is called *exploring alternatives.* You can explore alternatives with your child.

"Talking It Through": Five Steps for Exploring Alternatives

No matter who owns a problem, exploring alternatives is done in the same way. Follow these five steps:

1. **Understand the problem.** Make sure the problem is clear to both you and your child. Use reflective listening. Ask questions that help you understand. Explain the problem clearly and respectfully. State your own feelings with I-messages: "When you _____ , I feel _____ because _____ ."

2. **Brainstorm ideas to solve it.** To brainstorm, ask your child for ways to solve the problems. Suggest your own ideas too. You can help by saying, "What might happen if you _____?"

These ideas are the *alternatives.* Stay open-minded for this step. Sometimes ideas sound silly or impossible. Don't be quick to judge them. One "silly" idea might help you or your child think of another really good one. For now, just think of *any* ideas.

3. **Discuss the ideas.** Now is the time to consider the ideas. Both you and your child should feel free to "try on" the different ideas. If you don't agree with an idea, challenge it respectfully. Don't say, "I'm sure that idea won't work." Instead say, "I worry that sticking to that plan will be hard for you." This clearly gets your concerns across to your child.

4. **Choose an idea.** Pick an idea you can both accept.

5. **Use the idea.** Agree to test the idea you have accepted. Decide together how long to use it. Plan enough time to give the idea a fair test.

Also, set a time to discuss if the idea is working. If it isn't, you can repeat the steps for exploring alternatives. Or you can try another idea from the first time you brainstormed.

Use Open Questions

When you talk with your child, you will need to ask questions. You want to ask *open* questions, not *closed* questions.

Closed Questions Stop the Discussion

Closed questions have *one* answer only—there is no room for discussion. Some closed questions can be answered only yes or no.

Other closed questions blame or criticize:

- "Do you think we're made of money?"
- "Don't you think you should do your homework?"
- "Why did you do that?"
- "Are you ever going to behave?"

Open Questions Keep Things Going

Open questions invite your child to keep talking. They show respect. They show that you want to listen:

- "How could you earn some money?"
- "What makes the homework hard?"
- "How do you feel about that?"
- "What would you rather do?"

Children are more likely to cooperate when they:

- feel respected
- have some control
- have a choice

Exploring Alternatives: Two Examples

Let's look at two examples of exploring alternatives. The first is for a problem the parent owns. The second is for a problem the child owns.

Coming Home on Time

It's summer. The kids on Luis's block like to play outdoors at night. Mom wants Luis to come in before dark. She knows it isn't safe for him to be out after dark. But Luis thinks it is safe.

This problem belongs to Mom. She decides to explore alternatives with Luis.

1. Understand the problem.

Mom starts. She says, "Luis, we have a problem. When you stay out after dark, I worry about you. It's not safe." Luis says, "It's safe—I'm not a baby."

Mom uses reflective listening. She says, "You feel I'm protecting you too much." Luis says, "But, Mom, playing is the most fun when it's a little dark. And it's not even dark when you call me in at 8:30!"

Then Mom explains her feelings: "I know you are a responsible boy, Luis. But after dark, some rough people come out. And there's lots of car traffic. I worry that somebody could hurt you.

Steps for Exploring Alternatives

1. **Understand the problem.**
2. **Brainstorm ideas to solve it.**
3. **Discuss the ideas.**
4. **Choose an idea.**
5. **Use the idea.**

Or that a car might hit you. You know just last month there was a bad accident."

2.   Brainstorm ideas to solve it.

Mom says, "Let's think of some ways we could solve this problem. Do you have any ideas?" Luis says, "What if I play right in front of the apartment?" Mom says, "That's one idea. What else?"

Luis and Mom think of some other ideas. Luis suggests staying out until 9:30. Mom suggests coming inside to finish playing.

3.   Discuss the ideas.

Luis and his mom talk about each idea. Luis thinks coming inside won't be fun. He thinks playing in front of the apartment isn't as good as the park. Mom thinks 9:30 is too late. She agrees that it's really not quite dark at 8:30.

4.   Choose an idea.

Mom and Luis find an idea they both think might work: Luis can play at the park until 8:30. Then he and his friends can play in front of the apartment until 9:00. Luis and Mom write an agreement. It looks like this:

> Luis agrees to come home by 8:30.
> Mom agrees that he may play out in front until 9:00. Luis agrees to come inside at 9:00. If he is late, then he will stay inside the next night.
>
> Luis   Mom

5.   Use the idea.

Mom says, "Let's follow this agreement for a few nights. We'll see how it works. Then we can talk about it again. When should we talk again?" Luis says, "I don't know." Mom says, "Let's use it for the next three nights. On Friday, we can talk again."

If Luis follows the plan, the problem is solved. But what if Luis comes home late? The next night, Mom can say, "By coming home yesterday later than we agreed, you decided to stay inside tonight. You can try again tomorrow."

Open questions invite your child to keep talking. They show respect.

- "Tanisha may spend the night if you agree to stay out of your sister's makeup."

Let Your Child Learn From Consequences

When you need to correct your child's behavior, you can use a *consequence*. A consequence is the result of a choice the child has made.

Some Consequences Just Happen

Consequences that just happen because of an action are called *natural consequences.*

- If Liz doesn't eat supper, she'll be hungry by bedtime.

- If Drew doesn't wear a raincoat or bring an umbrella, he'll get wet in the rain.

- If Sachi plays too roughly with her dog, the dog may nip her.

Create Logical Consequences Too

Some natural consequences aren't safe. Also, many behaviors aren't covered by natural consequences. In these cases, you will need to create *logical* consequences:

On Monday, Mom saw Kayla riding her bike with no hands. Mom told Kayla, "Riding with no hands isn't safe. You could lose control. Then you could be hit by a car. You can ride your bike safely or walk to your friend's. You decide."

Kayla agreed to ride safely. But on Tuesday, Mom saw her goofing off again on the bike. Mom said, "I see you've decided to walk. You can bike again on Thursday."

What Makes a Consequence Different From Punishment?

Here are some ways consequences are different from punishment:

- They show respect for both you and your child.

- They fit the misbehavior.

- They are for bad choices—not bad kids.

- They are about now—not the past.

- They are firm and friendly.

- They allow choice.

Thinking About Limits

Limits are important. For example:

- A parent might keep the home quiet from 7:00 to 8:00 at night. The TV is off. In this quiet time, the child can do homework. The parent can read, work, and be there to help the child.

- A parent can negotiate a regular bedtime with the child. The child goes to the bedroom at that time. The parent can't force the child to go to sleep. Even so, the child has a limit—to be in the bedroom.

Think of some other limits that might help your child.

Consequences Show Respect

Consequences show respect—for *both* you and your child:

You are trying to sleep before going to your second job. Your child has the TV blaring. He is laughing with delight. You don't yell at him to "turn it off or else." You say, "Sounds like a funny program. But I need my sleep. Please turn it down or find something else to do."

Consequences "Fit"

Consequences make sense. They fit the misbehavior.

Rico leaves a mess all over the house. His mom doesn't say, "No movie for you on Saturday!" Going to a movie has nothing to do with leaving a mess. Instead, Mom says, "Let's keep the place clean. Please pick up your stuff. Otherwise, I'll put all your stuff that's not picked up in a bag. I'll put the bag away for three days."

Effective discipline fits the misbehavior.

Consequences Are About Behavior

Consequences are for bad choices—not "bad" kids. You may have heard the phrase, "Separate the deed from the doer." Consequences help you do this. It is the misbehavior—not the child—that needs to be fixed! Consequences tell your child, "I don't like what you're doing, but I still love you":

Fiona used her dad's tools without asking. They got all mixed up. The hammer got lost. Her dad didn't say, "Fiona! You never put my stuff away. Now you've lost my hammer!" Instead, he said, "Please help me organize these tools again. You need to find where you left the hammer."

Consequences Are About *Now*

Consequences are about now—not the past.

Chris went to his friend's after school. He was supposed to be home by 5:00 to start homework. He got home at 6:00. His grandpa didn't say, "You're always late! How many times do we have to go through this? You're not going anywhere for a week, period!"

Instead, Grandpa said nothing right then. He did not get into a power struggle. He knew that Chris had made a choice: to come home late. The next day, Chris wanted to go to his friend's again. Grandpa said, "I'm sorry, but you're not ready to be responsible to come home on time. You'll have to come straight home today. We'll give it another try tomorrow."

Consequences Are Firm and Friendly

Consequences are firm and friendly. They show respect and caring.

Bobby really wanted a puppy. He agreed to take care of it. Today when Mom comes home, she finds a hungry puppy. There is no fresh water. The puppy has wet the floor.

Mom takes care of the puppy. Later, Bobby wants to show his friends the puppy. The children want to play with it. Mom doesn't say, "You did not feed Fluffy! And you didn't walk her after school! So you may not play with her today!" Instead, she speaks in a matter-of-fact voice. She says, "No, Bobby—you haven't taken care of feeding and walking Fluffy today. We'll try again tomorrow."

Consequences Allow Choice

With a choice, the child has some control.

When his sons fight at the table, Dad doesn't say, "You two knock it off right now or you'll go to bed without supper." Instead, he says calmly, "Settle down or leave the table until you're ready to join us. You decide."

How Can I Use Consequences With My Child?

Here are some guidelines for using consequences.

Be Both Firm and Kind

Firm and *strict* do not mean the same thing. To be strict is to show that you are the boss. To be firm is to show that you expect

---

How to Set Consequences

1. **Give choices.** Plan to accept whatever choice your child makes, within your limits.

2. **Follow through.** Allow the consequence to happen. Tell your child there will be a chance to change the choice later.

3. **Add more time.** If your child misbehaves again, the child must wait longer before trying again.

cooperation and respect yourself. Your voice shows kindness. You show firmness by following through with consequences.

Grace wanted Therese to stay overnight. Mom said, "Therese may stay if you both agree to go to bed by nine o'clock." At 9:15, Grace and Therese are still playing noisily. Mom says, "It looks like you've decided that Therese will go home. I'll call her dad to come get her."

Mom let the decision stand. She did not criticize the girls' choice. Mom could have done other things. There may have been no way to get Therese home at 9:15. Then Mom could have separated the girls. Children often learn powerful lessons when they experience consequences. Expect your children to learn from their "mistakes."

Talk Less, Act More

Children quit listening when parents talk too much. The best time for talk is when you and your child are calm. When you use consequences, talk as little as possible as you follow through with action.

Effective discipline shows that you expect cooperation.

Don't Fight or Give In

Set limits and let your child respond to them. Then accept your child's decision. You aren't in a contest, and you don't have to "win." The goal is to help children be responsible for their own behavior.

Kavon asked Mom if he could go to a movie with Malik on Saturday. Mom said he could go if he finished his homework. Kavon agreed. At 1:00 on Saturday, Malik came to get Kavon. Mom asked to see Kavon's finished homework. Kavon said, "I'll do it tonight." Mom said, "I'm sorry, Kavon, but since your homework isn't done, you'll have to miss the movie."

Kavon began to beg. He said, "Aw, Mom, there's nothing to do tonight. I can finish then." "No," said Mom. "We agreed it'd be done before the movie." "Please, Mom!" cried Kavon. "I promised Malik I'd go with him. <u>Please</u> let me go."

Mom said no more. She simply left the room. She heard Kavon complain to Malik. She heard him stomp around the kitchen after Malik had left. But she didn't say any more about it to her son.

Mom didn't fight or give in. She let her son decide how to respond to the limits. Kavon didn't finish his homework. So Mom knew he had decided not to go to the movie. Kindly and firmly, she followed through with discipline related to the behavior.

Use Respectful Words

When giving a choice, use a friendly and helpful tone. One way is to say: "You may _____ or _____. You decide."

- "You may eat with us politely or you may leave the table. You decide."
- "You can follow the bus rules or walk home from school. You decide."

Another way is to use the words "You may _____ if _____."

- "You may have Caitlin and Stephanie over if you agree not to shut your sister out of the room."
- "You can make pizzas if you leave the kitchen as clean as you found it."

Respect the Choice

Your child may choose the consequence as a way of testing if you mean what you say.

When this happens, accept your child's choice. Simply say, "Your behavior tells me you've chosen to _____." Or, "I see you've decided. You can try again tomorrow." Keep your voice, face, and body respectful.

If You're Having Trouble

If you find it hard to use consequences, check that you:

- Show an "open" attitude. Give the choice and accept your child's decision.
- Use a friendly tone of voice.
- Make sure the consequence fits the misbehavior.
- Stay consistent and follow through.

Negotiating Consequences

With older children, negotiating consequences is important. They are more likely to follow consequences they have helped decide. Ask what they think would be fair or what they would do if they were the parent. If the child refuses to help decide or chooses unreasonable consequences, you will need to set the consequence.

At times, negotiation isn't needed. Maybe the problem is too small, or too serious, with limited choices. There will be many opportunities to involve your child in negotiating consequences.

Make It Clear When There Isn't a Choice

Lots of times parents will offer a choice they don't really mean. If there really is no choice, don't hint that there is. This just sets the stage for problems. Instead, be clear about what you expect.

Dad took his kids to the city pool. He had to go to work at six. He could not be late. 5:00 would be time to leave so he could clean up and get to work on time.

Dad didn't say, "Time to go home—okay?" "Okay" seems like a choice. And he didn't say, "Are you ready to go home?" Hearing this, the kids might say, "No, not yet."

Instead, at 4:50 Dad said, "We need to leave in ten minutes." At 5:00, he said, "Time to go. Let's dry off."

If the children didn't come willingly, Dad could offer a choice: "You can come on your own, or I'll escort you out of the pool and we'll have to skip next weekend. You decide."

If his children don't cooperate, Dad will need to follow through. As he escorts the children from the pool, he can say, "We'll try again next weekend."

Let All Children Be Responsible

Often a problem occurs in a group of children. Parents can't always know who misbehaved. If this happens, don't try to find the guilty person. And don't listen to tattling. Have the children decide how to handle the problem:

Rebecca had three children aged 8, 9, and 11. Rebecca was at home in the late afternoons. Her children often brought friends to watch TV. When the kids left, Rebecca always found apple cores, cups, candy wrappers, and crumbs all over the living room. One afternoon she told the children, "If you want to snack while you watch TV, you will need to clean up after yourselves."

That night, Rebecca found some of the mess cleaned up—but not all of it. She didn't play detective. Instead, she decided not to let the children snack in the living room the next day. She believed the kids could work it out together. They could decide how to earn back the privilege of snacking in the living room.

What Makes Sense?
Use discipline that "fits" the misbehavior—that makes sense. This means that each consequence will be different. It will depend on the misbehavior. For example:

If your child won't eat supper, you don't send the child to bed. Going to bed has nothing to do with eating. Instead, accept what the child chooses to eat of what is served. You might say, "This is what we're having tonight. Our next meal is breakfast."

Remember, you are not trying to *make* your child eat. You are teaching your child to make and learn from choices.

Don't Worry About What Others Think

Sometimes children push the limits in front of other people. This is a way of testing parents. It is important to follow through:

Phen and Nick are 10. They are on the same ball team. Phen's dad sat with Nick's mom at his son's ball game. After the game, the boys wanted to go to a movie.

Nick's mom offered to drive them and pick them up. Dad asked Phen, "What movie?" "Night Terror!" said Phen. Dad said, "No, that movie is too violent, Phen. You guys can pick a different one." "Aw, Dad," said Phen. "That's not fair. Nick already saw it once, and he says it's awesome. Please? Please?"

Nick's mother said to Dad, "I saw it with Nick, and I didn't think it was too bad." "Yeah, Dad," cried Phen. "C'mon—don't treat me like a baby." But Dad stayed firm. He said to Nick's mom, "It's nice of you to take the boys to a movie. But I don't want Phen to see this one. He can pick another movie or stay home tonight." "No fair!" shouted Phen. "If Nick can go, why can't I?"

Dad said calmly, "I see you've decided to come home tonight, Phen. Get your glove and cap and let's go."

Standing firm when another parent questions you is not easy. But the message to your child is a strong one. Your limits are clear and consistent.

Sometimes parents find their child's behavior embarrassing. They think it shows something bad about the parents. But children won't always act as we wish they would. When they don't, it's not always because of us.

Stay Calm

Yelling, nagging, or making threats turn a consequence into punishment. Keep calm. Be both kind and firm. Show respect for yourself and your child.

If you do get angry and find it hard to stay calm, *wait*. Say nothing. Get away to a different room to cool down. If you can't

The goal of discipline is to teach children self-discipline.

Practicing How to Say It

When you give a consequence, your purpose is to let the child learn. Three things are important:

- your tone of voice
- your body language
- the words you choose

Think about a problem with your child. Think of respectful words for giving a choice. Practice in front of the mirror.

Other parents may not approve of your approach to discipline.

Encouragement STEP

Notice when your child tries to do something positive. Focus on effort. Give encouragement. For example:

- "You spent a lot of time doing that."
- "It feels good to make progress."
- "Looks like this part is off to a good start."

Notice especially when your child tries to cooperate.

leave the room, say to your child, "I'm too angry to talk right now. We will need to talk about this later." Take deep breaths and think about a way to give a choice when you've calmed down. Then notice positive behavior soon after you've corrected the misbehavior. This helps separate the deed from the doer.

Be Patient

Consequences cut down on but don't get rid of future misbehavior. That may take time. You are changing your patterns of behavior. Your child may be testing your limits. Remember this:

$$\text{PATIENCE} + \text{PRACTICE} = \begin{array}{l}\text{PROGRESS FOR YOU} \\ \text{AND YOUR CHILD}\end{array}$$

When Parents Don't Agree

Parents don't always agree on discipline. If this is true of your family, the parents need to deal with the children in their own way. Fighting about discipline isn't good for your children. They will adjust to each parent's way. Model cooperation and mutual respect as best you can.

Stepchildren may not accept discipline from a stepparent. Unless problems happen between a stepparent and stepchild, leaving discipline to the birth parent is best. With improving relationships, the stepparent can move into an equal discipline role with the birth parent.

You Have Taken Another Big Step

In Chapter 6, you have learned a way of discipline that makes sense:

- You have looked at the differences between punishment and discipline.
- You have learned a way to set limits and give choices.
- You have seen that you can discipline your child by showing respect and firmness.
- You have thought about choices you could give your child.
- You have seen the importance of patience and consistency.

THIS WEEK

Choose *one* discipline problem to work on. Don't start with the hardest one! Think of consequences you could use. Think of what to say and do when you offer choices. Be consistent, friendly, and firm. Follow through with your consequences.

For Your *Family*

Continue with family meetings. Discuss consequences for broken agreements. When discussing consequences, say, "We all forget sometimes. What should happen if someone forgets an agreement we've made?" The children may come up with punishing ideas, such as "Spank them." If this happens, tell the children you're not comfortable with that solution and brainstorm more ideas. For chores, many families decide to set a rule of "work before fun." Before people do fun activities, their chores need to be done. The rule applies to parents as well as children.

JUST FOR YOU

The Rights of Parents and Children

Parents and children have rights. Centering your life on your children is not fair to you or your child.

As a parent, you have the right to:

- friendships
- privacy
- time for yourself
- respect for your property
- a life apart from your children

Your child has the right to:

- be raised in a safe and loving home
- friendships outside the family
- privacy
- respect for property

These rights can be summed up in one phrase: *mutual respect.*

This week, look for ways to maintain your rights. What will you do to show respect for your child's rights?

POINTS TO REMEMBER

1. Discipline helps children learn to cooperate. It helps them learn self-control.

2. The keys to effective discipline are:
   - Show respect for your child and yourself.
   - Expect your child to cooperate.
   - Provide choices.
   - Apply consequences.

3. Instead of giving orders, set limits and give choices. Limits and choices give everyone some control.

4. A consequence happens when a child makes a choice. Consequences are a way to set limits and give choices. Consequences:
   - show respect for you and your child
   - fit the misbehavior
   - are for bad choices, not bad kids
   - are about now, not the past
   - are firm and friendly
   - allow choice

5. To use consequences, give choices. Then follow through by letting the child act on the choice.

6. Some guidelines for using consequences are:
   - Be both firm and kind.
   - Talk less, act more.
   - Don't fight or give in.
   - Use respectful words.
   - Respect the choice.
   - Make it clear when there is no choice.
   - Let all children be responsible for their choices.
   - Don't worry about what others think.
   - Stay calm.

7. Be patient with yourself and your child.

Chart 6
CONSEQUENCES AND DAILY ROUTINES

Time of Day	Activity or Problem	Choices (Keep respectful tone)	Consequences
Morning	Getting up on time	"You may get up on time or go to bed earlier."	If child gets up late: Goes to bedroom earlier that night.
		"You can set your alarm and get up on time or miss breakfast. You decide."	If child gets up late: Misses breakfast.
	Eating breakfast	"You may eat breakfast or pack a healthy snack."	If a child misses breakfast: Takes healthy snack.
	Having things ready for school	"You may get up in time to pack your lunch or pack it the night before."	If child doesn't pack lunch: Goes without or uses allowance to buy own lunch.
			If child forgets or loses lunch money: Goes hungry that day.
		"I leave for work before you're up. I can sign your field trip slip the night before."	If child doesn't get permission slip signed: Does not go on field trip.
After School	TV	"You may watch TV for one hour, either after school or after supper."	Once limit is reached: Parent turns off TV.
		"You can watch shows we've agreed to or find something else to do."	If child argues or watches "off limits" program: Parent turns off TV. Child finds something else to do.
	Homework	"You may do your homework after school or after supper. You decide."	Child does homework before or after supper. If child does not do homework: Does homework after school next day.
		"I can pick you up at the library at five, or you can walk home."	Child is on time or walks home.
Evening	Phone	"You may talk on the phone after you've finished your homework."	If child uses phone before homework: May not use phone rest of that night.
		"You can do homework on the phone if you can be off in twenty minutes."	When limit is reached: Parent respectfully interrupts child to end phone call.
		"Please limit phone calls to ten minutes, or talk to your friends at school."	
	Kitchen chores	"Please do the dishes, or we'll run out of clean ones."	If a child does not wash dishes: Parent allows dishes to pile up.
	Activities	"You can sign up for baseball or soccer. You decide."	If child doesn't choose: Does not sign up for either, or parent chooses for child.
		"You may play in band if you agree to practice. It's up to you."	If child does not practice: Parent returns instrument to school or rental store.
		"You can go to the mall if Ted's dad or older sister goes too."	If child goes to mall without adult: May not go to mall. Parent sets time when child can try again.
	Bedtime	"You may go to bed or do something quiet in your room."	If child plays or reads until too late in room: Has natural consequence of being tired in morning.
		"You can head for bed, or I can walk you there. You decide."	If child doesn't go to bed on own: Parent takes child to bedroom.

Choosing *Your* Approach

You have learned four ways to help your child choose better behavior:

- **Use reflective listening.** This is helpful when your child owns the problem.
- **Use I-messages to tell how you feel.** I-messages help when you own the problem.
- **Explore alternatives.** You can do this no matter who owns the problem.
- **Give choices.** The choice depends on who owns the problem.

How Can I Decide What to Do?

Which approach you use will depend on what is happening. Sometimes you will use only one. Sometimes you will use them all.

Emilio, 11, left his things all over the place. Shoes, baseball cards, books, and food wrappers were everywhere. Mom used an I-message: "When things aren't picked up, I feel frustrated. I like to come home to a pleasant place." Emilio said, "I know. I'm sorry. I'll do better." "Good," said Mom. "Thank you."

That night, Emilio picked up most of his things and took them to his room. The next day, though, he began leaving them around again. Mom decided to explore alternatives at a family meeting. She said, "Emilio, when our agreements aren't kept, I feel like I don't count around here." Emilio said, "Why does everything have to be perfect?"

Here's what you will learn . . .

- **The approach you use depends on the situation.**
- **To decide what to do, ask yourself what the child's goal is, who owns the problem, what your purpose is, and how you can best help.**
- **With schoolwork, your job is to help your child be ready and able to learn.**
- **You can expect your children to get along together and solve problems among themselves.**
- **You can use your STEP skills and approaches to help your child avoid serious safety problems.**

Mom used reflective listening. She said, "You're angry because you think I'm unreasonable about wanting a neat home?" "Yeah," said Emilio. "I like it when things are kind of messy. It feels comfortable." Dad said, "Emilio, Mom and I work hard to keep our home clean and neat. We like to come home to a pleasant place." "But it's my home too," said Emilio. "And I hate getting nagged at all the time." Mom said, "It looks like we need to find a way for all of us to feel comfortable. What do you think we can do?"

Emilio and his parents brainstormed ideas. They agreed on a plan: After school, Emilio would relax for half an hour. Then he would pick up his things. Mom and Dad would not nag. As long as the living room, bathroom, and kitchen were neat, Emilio could keep his own room as messy as he liked. They agreed to test the plan for a week.

For two days, Emilio picked up his things. But soon he began leaving them around again. Mom and Dad said nothing to Emilio about it. At the end of the week, Dad said, "How do you think our plan is working?" Everyone looked at the messy living room. Emilio said, "It's hard to pick up all the time. I'm tired after school."

Mom asked for Emilio's ideas on solving the problem. He didn't offer any. Mom stayed friendly. At the same time, she was firm. She said, "Emilio, you seem to feel picked on because we want you to keep our agreement. But Dad and I have a right to a clean home. You have a choice: You can pick up as we agreed. Or, I'll pick up and keep the things I find until you show you're ready to pick your things up. You decide."

Emilio got mad. He shouted, "You can't keep my stuff!" Dad stayed calm. He asked Emilio, "Do you have any other ideas to solve this problem?" "No!" shouted Emilio. "You can't keep things that belong to me!" Mom and Dad didn't say more. They got up quietly and left to go for a walk.

These parents needed to use all of the approaches to deal with Emilio's behavior. You can see that they used them a little at a time.

First, Mom used an I-message. Mom's I-message might have solved the problem. Then, a few days later, Mom could say: "Emilio, I appreciate how you've been picking up your things." But Mom's I-message didn't solve the problem. So Mom added another approach.

Mom used reflective listening. Mom's reflective listening showed Emilio that she respected his feelings and expected him to cooperate. The problem might have ended after that. But it didn't. Mom and Dad decided to add another approach.

The family explored alternatives. Dad and Mom stayed respectful. They asked Emilio for his ideas. When he didn't give any, they came up with their own. They brainstormed ideas and agreed to a plan. If Emilio had kept the agreement, the problem would have been solved. But Emilio didn't stick to the agreement. Mom and Dad decided to use discipline that made sense.

Mom and Dad gave Emilio a choice. Mom and Dad were friendly but firm. When Emilio argued, they refused to join in a power struggle.

What if Emilio still doesn't pick up? Then Mom and Dad will need to do what they said they would do.

Dad and Mom will need to follow through. Dad and Mom will need to keep the things Emilio leaves lying around. Soon, Emilio will lose a special baseball card or an important school paper. Then he might start picking up.

Emilio still needs encouragement. Mom and Dad need to find ways to encourage Emilio when he is not misbehaving. How?

- by noticing Emilio's efforts
- by showing Emilio that they appreciate him
- by asking for Emilio's help
- by asking Emilio to join in making family decisions

All these things are ways that Emilio's parents can help their son choose better behavior.

It will take time. If Mom and Dad don't give up, their relationship with Emilio should improve. Over time, they may find that they need to use consequences less and less. Emilio will have more respect for them. He'll know that they will use a consequence if they need to. He may decide to change his behavior before a consequence happens.

Deciding What to Do

Whenever there is a problem with your child, begin by deciding who owns the problem. Ask yourself:

1. Are my rights being disrespected?
2. Could anybody get hurt?
3. Are someone's belongings threatened?
4. Is my child too young to be responsible for this problem?

- If the answer to *any* of these questions is yes, then you own the problem.
- If the answer to *every* question is no, then your child owns the problem.

If Your Child Owns the Problem

If your child owns the problem, you might do one of the following: decide to ignore it, use reflective listening, or offer to explore alternatives for solving the problem.

If You Own the Problem

If you own the problem, decide what your child's goal is. Notice how you feel. Respond in a way that your child does not expect. Think about your purpose:

- Do you want to give attention, or help your child be self-reliant?
- Do you want to show who's the boss, or help your child be independent and responsible?
- Do you want to get even, or show that you understand?
- Do you want to let your child off the hook, or help your child be self-confident?

Depending on the problem, ignore the misbehavior. Use I-messages to tell how you feel. Explore alternatives to resolve conflicts. If you need to, offer choices and let your child learn from the consequences. Be both firm and respectful.

Thinking About What to Do

Think about a problem you have at home with your child. Decide who owns the problem. Think about your purpose. Decide how you can best help. Ask yourself:

- **What is my child's goal?**
- **Can I ignore this misbehavior?**
- **Can I use reflective listening? Can I use an I-message?**
- **Can we explore alternatives?**
- **Can I give a choice?**
- **How can I encourage my child?**

Plan a way to solve the problem with the child.

Effective discipline needs to fit the misbehavior.

When Children Forget Chores

Parents may think that not giving children an allowance when they don't do chores is a consequence. What do children learn? That they should be paid to contribute to the family.

Children have a right to share in the family's money. They also need to help out. At family meetings, talk about what should happen if people forget chores. Maybe you'll agree on a rule of "work before fun."

If chores still aren't done, use "task trading." You say you will do children's chores. Then you won't have time to do other things for them, such as drive them to activities. List what you do for them. Discuss which ones will go undone if you do children's chores. Make the tasks being traded as equal as possible. Don't use task trading as a weapon. Discuss chores at the next family meeting. At that time, the children can decide if they want to do their chores. If not, continue task trading.

What About Schoolwork?

School is the child's responsibility. Does this mean you should never help your child with schoolwork? No. To succeed in school, your child needs your support.

Set the Stage

Here are some things you can do to help your child be able to succeed in school:

Give your child healthy food. A healthy diet helps your child's body *and* mind.

Encourage exercise. Every day, your child could get some exercise. It helps develop the body and mind. It helps your child deal with stress. Moderate exercise, such as walking, can become a family activity.

Build your child's self-esteem. Give as much encouragement as you can. Children who feel good about themselves are eager to learn.

Teach responsibility. Help your child learn to be responsible at home. Children can do chores. They can make choices within limits and experience the results of their decisions. Responsibility at home will help build responsibility in school.

School Is a Team Effort

Think of your child's learning as a team effort. The team members are the teacher, the child, and you:

- The teacher's job is to teach.
- The child's job is to learn.
- The parent's job is to help the child be ready and able to learn.

Be involved with the school. Meet your child's teacher. Go to parent-teacher conferences. Take part in school activities. Most schools have an organization for parents and teachers. Join it. Volunteer to be a room parent or to help with a school event.

Join a parenting group. Talking with other parents in a parenting group helps. This is a good way to build your skills and your confidence. As you do, you will become a better and better parent. Working with your child will be easier. If you're reading this book on your own, consider joining a STEP parenting group.

Avoid Rewards and Punishment

Some parents pay children for good grades. Grades are not as important as learning. If children start to expect money for grades, they may focus on money, not on learning. They may also lose the chance to enjoy the rewards of learning, hard work, and a job well done. These rewards come from inside the child.

Some parents punish children for low grades. Punishment does not help children learn to be responsible. Grounding a child, spanking, or taking away TV creates power struggles and discouragement, not cooperation.

Let Your Child Be Responsible

Some children handle homework on their own without any trouble. They set their own schedules and get the job done without fuss. Others may need you to help them build a homework routine.

- Give your child a choice of when to do homework.
- Make sure your child has a specific place to do homework.
- Be there to answer questions or review material with your child at the end of a study period.

If your child won't take responsibility, there will be consequences at school. Let your child experience these consequences. If you and the teacher feel you should help your child, use the skills such as encouragement and communication you have learned in STEP. If this doesn't help, offer choices.

- "You may study after school or after supper. Which do you choose?"
- "You can go to the movie Saturday if your homework is done as we agreed."

If your assistance or choices don't help, the child may be seeking power or revenge. Calmly tell your child, "I can't make you study.

I'll leave it up to you. You can ask me for help." Be firm with yourself to stay out of power contests. Realizing you can't force your child, what are your other choices? Eventually, if you really mean to leave it up to the child, the child will take responsibility.

Is your child really having trouble? Listen reflectively to learn more about what's going on. Talk about ways to get the needed help. Be sure to ask for your child's teacher's cooperation. Explain to the teacher the reasons for your action.

Be Encouraging

Some children do poorly in school to display inadequacy. Remember that a child who shows helplessness is extremely discouraged. It is important for you to:

- Notice and encourage every small step the child makes—in schoolwork and in other areas.
- Focus on the child's strengths.
- Tell your children you love them.

What About Other Problems?

For every problem, you can use the approaches you have learned in STEP. Let's look at some examples.

"I Won't Eat That"

Many children are fussy eaters. Most parents worry about what children eat and don't eat.

Ines is fussy about food. Most nights she eats only a small part of her supper. She says, "I don't like tomatoes. They're slimy." "I'm tired of chicken. Gross!" "Ick. What's in this casserole?"

Ines's parents wish she would eat supper. They worry that she won't get the nutrition she needs. They don't keep snacks like ice cream or chips around. Instead, they buy healthy snacks.

What Can Ines's Parents Do?
Ines owns the problem of being a fussy eater. Her parents can't make her eat her supper. That doesn't mean her parents can't help.

- Ines's parents can think about what her goal might be. If they feel annoyed, she may want attention. If they feel angry, Ines may want power. They can refuse to fight. They might simply ignore Ines's eating and her comments for a few days. They

Children who feel good about themselves are more likely to think for themselves.

can give Ines positive attention and encouragement at other times.

- Ines's parents could ask her what she would like to have for supper. This might be a good topic for a family meeting. They could agree on how often to fix something Ines asks for. They could even have her help fix it.
- Ines's parents might offer a choice. At suppertime, they could say: "Eat as much as you like. This is it until breakfast." If Ines is hungry for a few nights, she might decide to eat a healthier supper.

If Ines does not stay healthy, this problem will become her parents'. Some children go too far and eat very little. This can be extremely serious. If this happens, the parent needs to take the child for medical care.

When Is Food a Problem?

Children's bodies and eating habits vary. It isn't unusual for a child to dislike some foods or want to eat too many sweets. Sometimes eating becomes a problem. Seek medical help if your child:

- refuses to eat for fear of becoming fat
- feels "fat" when the child is actually thin
- eats way too much most of the time
- gains or loses a lot of weight quickly

When Brothers and Sisters Fight

Brothers and sisters often fight. This fighting is so common that many parents believe it is "normal." The parents *expect* brothers and sisters to fight. Children know what parents expect.

Leo and Adam fight a lot. In the morning, Adam pounds on the bathroom door. Leo stays in as long as he can, just to "get" Adam. In school, Adam makes fun of Leo. He embarrasses Leo in front of his friends. After school, they argue about who will do what chores. Leo calls Adam "dummy" and "pervert." Adam tries to eat up Leo's favorite snacks. Dad tries to get them to stop, but they keep fighting.

Dad is fed up with both boys. He feels bad that his children don't get along better but doesn't know what else to do. He thinks that most children in families fight.

Adam and Leo own the problem of getting along with each other. Parents' attempts to stop the fighting usually makes it worse. No matter what, at least one child will probably feel that the parent is taking sides.

Children's fighting usually has a goal. It might be to get the parent's attention. It might be to show the parent they can do what they want. One child might pick on another who seems to be the parent's "favorite."

What Can Dad Do?

- Dad can't make Adam and Leo get along better. But he can expect them to cooperate. He can also notice when they do cooperate. When he sees them getting along, he could say: "You two seem to be having fun." Or, "Looks like you have worked things out."

- Dad can refuse to get involved. If he does, Adam and Leo's fights may get worse before they get better. They may try to pull Dad back into the struggle by tattling. Dad could say: "This problem is for you and your brother to solve. I know you'll figure it out." This shows the boys that Dad believes they can get along. If they keep asking Dad to interfere, he can go to another room and close the door.

What if someone could get hurt? If there is hitting, biting, or kicking, the problem will become Dad's. Then he could use a consequence. He could say: "One of you might get hurt. You can either handle your problem without hitting or be separated until you can get along better." If the hitting continues, Dad will need to follow through and separate the children.

What if one child is much smaller? If a smaller child could get hurt, Dad will need to step in. For example, if Leo was 6 and Adam was 10, Dad could say: "Come on, Leo. Let's go find something else for you to do." This stops the fight. It doesn't punish either Adam or Leo.

What if boys and girls fight?
When boys fight with girls, many parents punish the boy. This is unfair and the boys may resent such treatment. In any fight, both boys and girls need to experience the consequences.

What About Lying and Stealing?

Sooner or later, most children will tell a lie. Many children will take something that does not belong to them. This does not mean the children will grow up to be liars or thieves. What should you do if your child steals something or tells a lie? Punishment and rewards can encourage lying. Handle it like other misbehavior. The child has made a choice to lie or steal. Now the child must experience the consequences.

Thinking About Children's Fights

Think about when your children argue. Ask yourself:

- **What do I usually do when my children fight? Does it help?**

- **What else can I do?**

Decide what you will do the next time your children fight. Stick to your plan.

Dulcee was sitting on the floor listening to a new tape. Her dad said, "I've never heard this tape before. When did you get it?" Dulcee mumbled, "A while ago." She didn't look at her dad. Dad said, "Is something wrong?" Dulcee looked at her feet. After a long minute, she said, "I stole it." Then she started to cry.

Dulcee took something that wasn't hers. She and her dad own this problem together.

What Can Dad Do?

Dad needs to follow through with discipline that makes sense. He could take Dulcee to the store where she stole the tape and find the manager. Dulcee will have to tell the manager what she has done. She will need to return the tape. The manager may also want Dulcee to pay for the tape. She may tell Dulcee she won't be allowed in the store anymore. Whatever the store decides to do, it is a consequence that Dulcee must accept.

A Word About Repeated Lying or Stealing

If a child begins a pattern of lying or stealing, the problem is more serious. Getting some help for your child is important.

What About Violence?

Violence is all around us. We see it on TV. We read about it in the newspaper. Many people live with violence in their homes. Parents worry about violence. The most important thing you can do about violence is to teach your child *nonviolence*.

Decide Not to Hit

Hitting is a form of violence. If children see that their parents hit, they may see that as the way to solve problems. Yelling can be violent too. If children hear their parents yell, they may decide that yelling gets them what they want.

Hitting and yelling won't solve problems. They will make problems worse. Pages 75-76 have more ideas about what to do when you feel like hitting or yelling.

Set Limits on TV

TV has lots of violence. If children watch violence every day, they might begin to think violence is okay. Give your child a choice of TV programs that are *nonviolent*. Talk with your child about why you are setting those limits. Watch some programs yourself to decide on your limits. Watch TV *with* your child too. If violence occurs, discuss it. Don't ignore violence, face it head-on. This is a good way to start talking about violence.

Children are often one step ahead of parents.

You may find that your child wants to talk to you. Children worry about violence too.

What About Gangs?

Zach is 10 years old. He was playing outside after school. Some older boys from a gang came over. They asked Zach to come talk to them. Zach ran home. Tonight, he tells his parents about what happened. "I know they'll ask me again," Zach tells them. "What can I do?"

This is a big problem. Gangs don't respect people's rights. Someone might get hurt. Zach is too young to figure this out alone.

What Can Mom and Dad Do?

Zach's parents need to listen to his feelings. He needs to know they are there for him. Still, that is not enough. Zach's parents can't make the world completely safe. There are things they can do to help Zach avoid gangs.

- They can tell Zach he did the right thing. Saying nothing to the older boys and coming home was a good choice.
- They can help Zach find the safest places to walk and play.
- They can talk about what Zach should do next time. As they talk, they can ask for Zach's ideas. They can also give Zach theirs. He may have some good ideas. He may also have some ideas that are not so good. His parents need to hear these so they can help him do the safest thing.

Zach's parents can also look for other ways to help keep Zach safe:

- There may be an after-school program at school, or at a community center.
- A church, synagogue, or mosque may be open as a safe place for kids to study and play.
- There may be programs through the police department.
- Suggest that Zach walk home with a group of friends.
- There may be groups of parents working to keep their children safe. Zach's parents could join a group like that. They could even start one.

Helping Children Avoid Gangs

Gangs are a serious problem. No one can make gangs simply go away. As parents, we can help our children avoid getting involved in gangs. We need to help them now, when they are young. We need to help them before they are old enough to think about being part of a gang. How?

Help our children feel loved. When we encourage our children, we help them feel loved. When we accept our children, we help them feel wanted. We all need to know that we are loved. Children need to feel this love when they are young. They will be less likely to look for love in a gang later on.

Help our children feel powerful. Children need to feel powerful in some way. One way to give children control is to offer choices. When children can make decisions, they feel this good kind of power. Later, they will be less likely to want to join a gang to get power.

Help our children feel needed. We can help our children know that they are important to us. We show this when we ask for their ideas or expect them to cooperate. We can tell our children, too, how much their help means to us. We can help our children feel important to their families now, when they are young. Then they will be less likely to seek out the "family" of a gang later on.

What About Drugs?

Children as young as elementary school age often know about drugs. Children can get drugs in many ways.

- They can get cigarettes and alcohol from older children. They can sneak them from their parents. Sometimes parents even offer children sips of wine or beer.
- They can take medicines like aspirin or cough syrup at home.

- They can sniff glue, paint thinner, and spray paint at home.
- They can get marijuana and other illegal drugs from other children. They can get drugs from dealers who prey on children.

You can't guarantee that your child won't use drugs. Still, you can do many things to help your child make good choices. The skills and approaches you have learned in STEP can help you with the following.

Build your child's self-esteem. Children who feel good about themselves are more likely to think for themselves. They are less likely to let friends talk them into using drugs.

Teach your child to make decisions and solve problems. Children who can do this are more likely to think about the *consequences* of using drugs.

Encourage healthy activities. Children can become involved in school activities such as sports or clubs. Your place of worship probably has healthy activities they can be involved in too. When possible, participate as a parent volunteer or attend their activities. Participate in healthy activities as a family: Go to the park, plan a picnic, go to a movie. Do something that everyone enjoys.

Talk to your child about drugs. Don't preach, just share. Listen to your child's ideas and worries about drugs. Answer your child's questions honestly.

Get to know the parents of your children's friends. Work with other parents to plan safe, fun activities that don't include drugs.

Have children walk in groups. Walking to and from school with friends helps children resist drug dealers.

Watch your own drug use. Legal drugs such as cigarettes and alcohol—even over-the-counter medicines—can be abused. Children learn a lot about drugs just by watching parents.

Learning More About It
Many booklets have been written for parents and children about drugs. The office at your child's school or local police department will have some. You can also learn more by calling the National Clearinghouse for Alcohol and Drug Information at 1-800-729-6686.

Thinking Ahead

Think about the future. Your child will need to make choices about many things. Here are a few:

- schoolwork
- fighting
- friendships
- drugs
- sex
- body care

What are some things you can do to help your child make good choices about these things?

Encouragement
STEP

Focus on your child's feelings. Work to understand the feelings as fully as you can. Show that you understand. To help yourself do this:

- **Notice your child's words, tone of voice, and actions.**
- **Think about what your child feels and believes.**
- **Listen reflectively.**
- **Stay on your child's topic. Respond only to what your child says.**
- **See the situation from your child's point of view.**

As often as you can, take the time to listen in this way. It shows your child that you care and understand.

You Have Taken Another Big Step

In Chapter 7, you have seen that you can use your STEP skills and approaches in many ways. Throughout STEP, you have learned many ways to help your child be responsible and cooperate. You help by:

- showing respect for your child and yourself
- understanding the goals of your child's behavior
- changing the way you respond
- expecting cooperation
- encouraging your child
- listening and talking about feelings
- setting limits and giving choices
- working together to solve problems

All of these skills and approaches take practice. Stick with it. Be patient with yourself and your child. When you have trouble, think again about your parenting goals:

- to raise a child who is happy, healthy, confident, cooperative, and responsible
- to build a strong, lifelong relationship with your child
- to help your child grow to be a responsible adult
- to raise a child who is loved and able to give love

What's Next?

The next step is up to you! You have many new understandings and skills. Practice and use these new skills to help your child be responsible and independent. Keep encouraging and helping your child, yourself, and your family. Most of all, enjoy your relationship with your child.

JUST FOR YOU

Owning Your Achievements

Completing a parenting book or course is an accomplishment. It indicates you are capable of considering new ideas and are willing to help yourself grow.

- What is new, different, and good in your family right now?
- What would you like for your children in one, five, and ten years?
- How can the ideas in this book, and your abilities, help you and your children in your journey?

Remember, focusing on what we haven't yet accomplished is easy. Knowing what we *have* accomplished is more important.

For Your *Family*

Keep having regular meetings. At your next meeting:

- **Talk about agreements you have made.**
- **Work together to solve problems.**
- **Make plans together.**
- **Let your children talk. Add your ideas a little bit at a time.**
- **Have fun!**

Remember, all family members need to feel that their ideas are important.

POINTS TO REMEMBER

1. The approach you use with your child depends on what is happening

2. To decide what to do, ask yourself who owns the problem, what your purpose is, and how you can best help.

3. With schoolwork, your job is to help your child be ready and able to learn. Do this by:
   - setting the stage
   - avoiding rewards and punishment
   - letting your child be responsible
   - being encouraging

4. Unless the problem is serious, let your child experience the consequences of not eating.

5. Expect your children to get along together and solve problems among themselves. Only step in if someone could get hurt.

6. If your child lies or steals, follow through with consequences.

7. To encourage nonviolence, decide not to hit and to set limits on violent TV programs.

8. To help your child avoid gangs, work to help your child feel loved, powerful, and needed.

9. To help your child make good choices about drugs:
   - Build your child's self-esteem.
   - Teach your child to make decisions.
   - Talk to your child about drugs.
   - Get to know your child's friends and their parents.
   - Watch your own drug use.
   - Encourage healthy activities.
   - Have children walk in groups.

10. You can't guarantee your child's safety. Use your STEP skills and approaches to help your child avoid serious problems and make good choices.

Chart 7
STEPS FOR DECIDING WHAT TO DO

1. **Identify the Goal of Misbehavior**

   Notice three things:
   - How you feel
   - What you do
   - How your child responds

2. **Decide Who Owns the Problem**

   Ask yourself:
   - Are my rights being disrespected?
   - Could anybody get hurt?
   - Are someone's belongings threatened?
   - Is my child too young to be responsible for this problem?

3. **Look at Your Purpose**

   Ask yourself:
   - Do I want to give attention? Or help my child be self-reliant?
   - Do I want to show who's the boss? Or help my child be independent and responsible?
   - Do I want to get even? Or show that I understand?
   - Do I want to let my child off the hook? Or help my child be self-confident?

4. **Choose an Approach**

   Do one, or combine approaches:
   - Ignore the misbehavior if this will help your child cooperate.
   - Use reflective listening.
   - Use I-messages to tell how you feel.
   - Don't punish. Offer choices and let your child experience the consequences.
   - Explore alternatives.

5. **Keep on Encouraging Your Child and Yourself**

   To help your child:
   - Use encouragement, not praise.
   - Love and accept your child.
   - Have faith in your child.
   - Appreciate your child.
   - Notice when your child tries or improves.

   To help yourself:
   - Have patience with yourself.
   - Remember that your child is not you.
   - Set realistic goals.
   - Use positive self-talk.
   - Be as healthy as you can.
   - Have a sense of humor.
   - Have the courage to be imperfect.

   To help your family:
   - Treat each other with respect.
   - Expect cooperation.
   - Use family meetings to solve problems and have fun.

INDEX

V

Values. *See* Family values
Violence, 128-30. *See also* Hitting; Yelling

W

Words for "happy" and "upset" feelings,
    70

Y

Yelling, 4-5, 35, 72-73, 94, 103-04, 111,
    128. *See also* Violence
You-messages, 73, 81
Youngest child, 30